Spinal Intelligence

—

Jenn Pilotti

An imprint of J&A Publishing
www.rethinkingbiomechanics.com & https://www.jennpilotti.com

ISBN: 979-8-9873395-3-4 (paperback)
ISBN: 979-8-9873395-4-1 (ebook)

Illustrations by Hester van Toorenburg
Design by Dmytro Pereli
Photography by Erin Fortin Photography

CONTENTS

A NOTE
BEFORE YOU BEGIN

The stories in this book are real, drawn from years of working with clients whose experiences shaped my thinking in meaningful ways. Out of respect for their privacy, all names and identifying details have been changed.

The exercises and ideas in these pages are offered as movement education—a way of exploring how your spine participates in everything you do. This book is not intended as medical advice, and nothing here should be taken as a substitute for the guidance of a qualified healthcare professional. All participation in the exercises that follow is voluntary. If you have a medical condition, a history of injury, or any concerns about beginning a movement practice, please consult your physician before starting this or any other exercise program.

Move with curiosity. Move with care. And when in doubt, ask someone who knows your body's specific history.

INTRODUCTION

When I first started working with people, teaching them exercises for strength and flexibility, I was 22. My clients were in their 40s, 50s, and 60s. It was the era of stability balls and Airex pads, a time when every exercise was supposed to be a core exercise because everyone needed more transverse abdominis strength or their low backs were surely going to buckle and explode.

I noticed early on that people had different ways of moving and that this idea of a "right" way to move and a "wrong" way to move didn't seem to be bearing out in real life.

I would watch as people came up the stairs to meet me, intrigued by what their body language said about how they felt in that moment. I learned to observe a person's energy level and when to tone down my naturally sunny disposition.

There's a lot more to a person than their core muscles. The interplay between the outside world and our internal response to it shapes how movement is produced.

Since I wanted to be able to consistently give people a positive movement experience, I went to work studying and learning. Like most people in my field, I began by learning all about how muscles create movement.

Except.

When I was working on my undergraduate degree, I took courses in neurology, physiology, and behavior. We studied the nervous system and the feedback loop of input to output. The muscles creating movement were a byproduct, not the initiator of movement. This meant that blaming muscles for aberrant movement patterns or aches and pains didn't make sense.

Eventually I landed on the importance of how the brain and the nervous system interact. When you can move in a variety of ways, you become flexible in how you approach tasks like stepping over a large log or moving an awkward piece of furniture. When you stress your muscles gradually, you get stronger and build stamina; as you feel stronger, you become more confident in how you move.

And when you sense and feel more of your body, your physical self becomes more clear in your mind's eye, allowing you to show up more fully in the world.

These are the ideas that formed spinal intelligence. Your spine is central to you. It connects your limbs to you. It houses the nerves that provide feedback from your body to your brain and from your brain to your body. Your feet propel you forward, but your spine integrates you, enabling you to dance, throw a ball, or run a marathon.

Spinal intelligence is the cultivated awareness of how your spine participates in every movement and the confidence to trust it.

Twenty-four years later, I still work with some of the same clients. I'm now the same age some of them were when we started together. What I have learned is that while injuries happen, the body is remarkably resilient. It's not fragile, and you can dramatically alter the experience of a movement or exercise based on how you approach it.

I wrote this for the people who have been told they need to fix their posture or that they have weak core muscles. It's for the person who feels a nagging sense of discomfort in their neck or behind their right shoulder blade that persists no matter how much they stretch. It's for the person who feels disconnected from their body, despite regularly exercising, as though something is missing.

As you read through these pages, I invite you to try some of the exercises with a sense of curiosity. Like so many things in life, the exercises aren't about the outcome. They are about the transition in between. The journey.

A brief note about Chapter One and the reflections:

If anatomy isn't your thing, feel free to skip Chapter One. It's an overview that is meant to provide a foundation of what things look like before we get into how things work.

Throughout the book, you will find reflection exercises. They aren't optional extras. They are part of the process. Self-reflection is how you learn. And learning is where the magic happens.

And with that, let's get started.

CHAPTER 1:
THE BEGINNING

Once upon a time, I was a young trainer, eager to know everything. My starting place was the spine. This was the early 2000s, when *core stability* and *core training* were all the rage.

I eagerly dove into learning how to create the perfectly timed contraction of the deep abdominal muscles. I studied the importance of keeping the spine still while moving the arms. I became obsessed with posture, trying to "fix" my imperfections so I would meet the standards set by more experienced colleagues, yoga teachers, chiropractors, and physical therapists—people who told me how I "should" be moving.

It wasn't long before my body felt terrible. I realized the prevailing ideas about what the core (and the spine) actually did weren't aligned with how human beings truly move.

That realization sent me down a different path—one that included earning a graduate degree, learning movement from people outside the worlds of fitness, yoga, and strength and conditioning, and studying a wide range of systems to find the common themes. Along the way, my chronic pain disappeared, I built a successful coaching business, and I developed a very different perspective on how the core functions and its role in movement.

This book introduces **Spinal Intelligence**, a way of viewing the spine and its role in movement. It won't give you six-pack abs, and while it might ease your back pain, it is not medical advice. I am not a doctor or a physical therapist. The exercises you'll encounter are designed to help you feel lighter and move more efficiently—not to fix or cure anything.

What you *will* find (and feel, if you engage with the program) is a deeper understanding of what the torso does when you move, along with a stronger sense of connection and awareness through the entire center of your body.

Let's dive in.

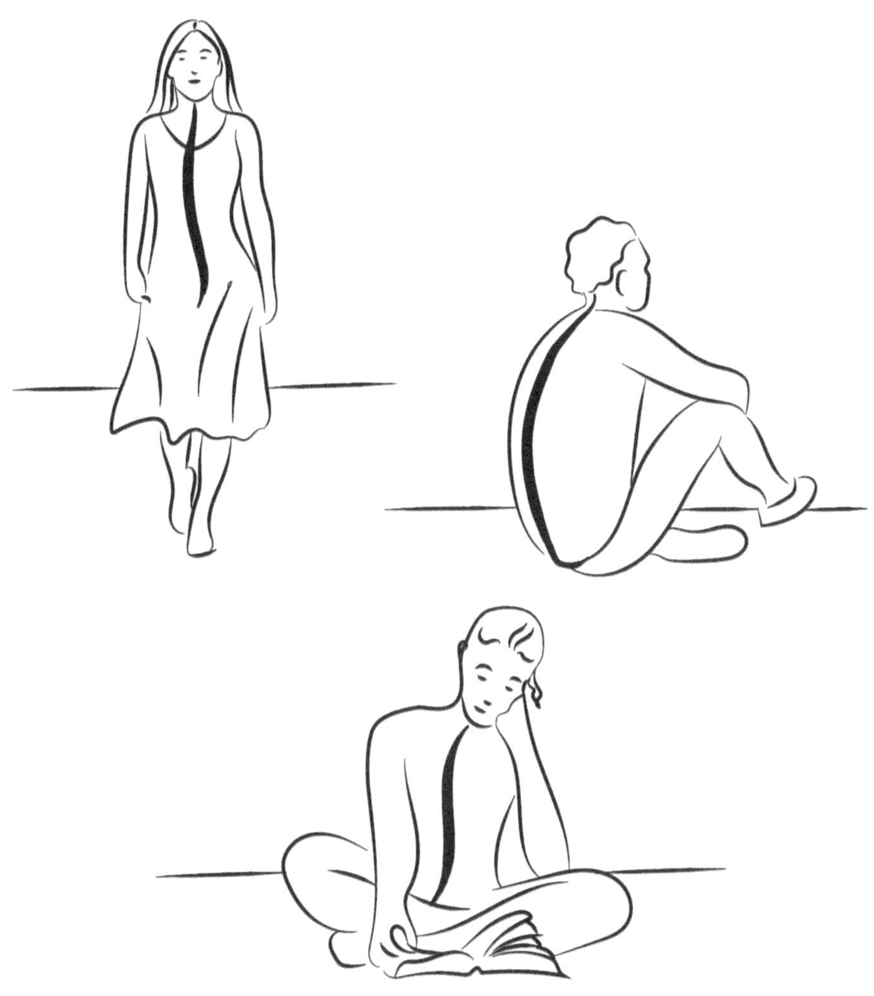

Have you ever watched slow-motion footage of professional sprinters?

If not, pull up a race on YouTube right now. (The 100-meter dash takes less than 11 seconds for women and less than 10 seconds for men—I promise I'll wait while you watch.)

NOW ASK YOURSELF:

» Did the spine move at all, or was it just the arms and legs?

(Watch again if you aren't sure. This is important.)

The spine isn't still—it's participating. Shirts shift. Bib numbers slide from center to side.

Now, watch an Olympic diver in slow motion.

Look closely at the torso. Does the spine rotate?

The answer is yes. Even though the diver enters the water in a perfectly vertical position to minimize splash, what happens between takeoff and entry involves significant spinal movement.

THE SPINE RESPONDS. THE SPINE INITIATES.

» The sprinter is propelled forward by the legs and arms—the spine responds.

» The diver rotates through the air—the spine helps initiate that rotation.

Both athletes demonstrate spinal movement.

If you look at the structure of the spine, this makes sense. The ends—the head and the low back—are designed for more mobility. The middle, where the ribs attach, still moves but to a lesser degree because:

1. Those vertebrae literally have a cage attached.

2. The back of the rib cage serves as an anchor for the arms, since the shoulder blades glide, rotate, and shift depending on arm motion.

The spine isn't a rigid column. It's more like a suspension bridge: bones supported by ligaments, muscles, and fascia. This design allows it to sway, adjust, and absorb load, while still providing strength and support to the rest of the body.

THE ANATOMY DISCUSSION

Here's the deal: before we dive further into how the spine works—and how you can begin tuning in to your spine working *for* you—we should talk about what it looks like under the skin.

If anatomy makes you squirm, feel free to skip this rudimentary introduction to your own structure.

If you peel away all of the layers covering the spine—skin, fascia, muscles, tendons, ligaments, nerves, arteries, and veins—you're left with a beautifully designed S-shaped column of bones.

At the very top of the S is your head. At the very bottom is your pelvis.

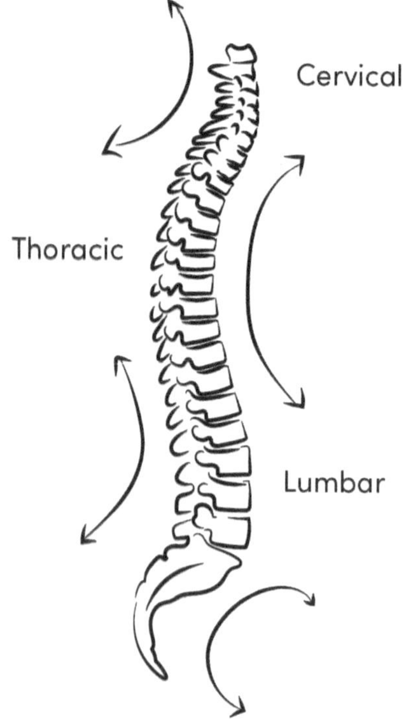

We are going to start with the neck, but these first couple of layers are consistent throughout the spine. Between the head and the ribcage are seven small bones called **vertebrae**. If you start counting from the top and move down the spine, you'll notice the vertebrae gradually get larger.

This makes sense—lower vertebrae bear more weight, so they need to be sturdier.

Between each vertebra sits a disc (except for between the first and second cervical vertebrae—that area is disc-free). Imagine this disc like a **water balloon between two sponges:** the top and bottom of the disc are spongy, and the center is soft and cushiony.

When you apply pressure—say, from movement or load—the disc compresses and redistributes the fluid, just like when you squeeze a water balloon. When you release the pressure, it rebounds to its original shape.

The disc works this way to absorb shock and help the spine move smoothly.

On each side of every vertebra is a small opening called an **intervertebral foramen** (Latin for "between the vertebrae opening"—anatomy names are often very literal).

If you add a layer to the bones, you'd see delicate **branches** emerging through these openings. These are **nerves,** the messengers that connect your central nervous system (the spinal cord and brain) to everything else (your peripheral nervous system).

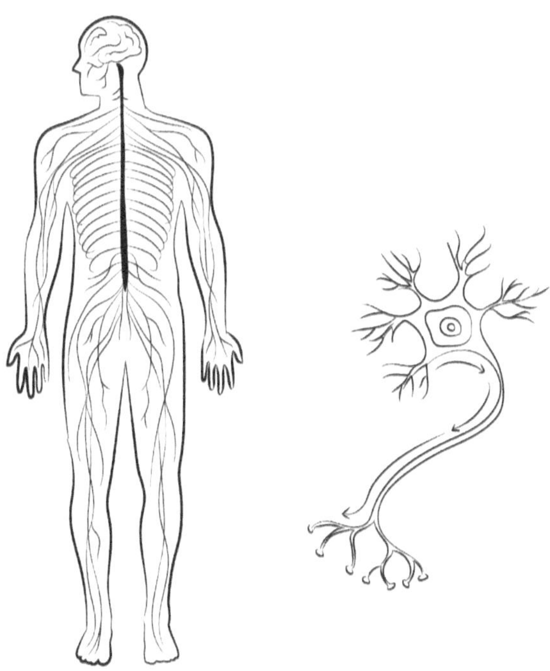

They help regulate things like heart rate and digestion, send electrical signals that tell your muscles to move, and gather information from your body about temperature, pressure, and position.

Because the nerves exit so close to the discs, if a disc isn't rebounding properly—maybe the fluid isn't redistributing, the outer layer has lost some of its sponginess, or pressure hasn't shifted in a while—this can cause the nerve to get compressed.

Think of it like **static or interference in a radio signal**—the signal gets distorted, which can lead to discomfort or miscommunication between the brain and body.

Next up: **ligaments.**

Ligaments are the **braided cables** of your body—tough, fibrous strands that connect bone to bone.

They're elastic, but only slightly, offering just enough give to allow motion without compromising stability. Think of them like the **tension bands of a suspension bridge**, supporting your structure even when unexpected forces, like a sudden step off a curb, jostle the system.

In the spine, ligaments run lengthwise along the front and back of the vertebral column, covering the vertebral bodies and discs. They also run between each vertebra, linking one to the next, like **zip ties** that keep the bones connected while still allowing some motion.

Some special ligaments in the cervical spine connect the head to the neck—just like there are unique vertebrae in this region that help support and move the head.

And now, we add another layer—one that anchors the head and enables movement:

MUSCLES.

But here's the cool thing about the body: there's not just one layer of muscle. There are multiple, like concentric rings, each contributing something different.

In the neck, muscles are grouped into three regions: **anterior** (front), **lateral** (sides), and **posterior** (back).

FRONT OF THE NECK:

The muscles in the front of the neck are further divided into three layers:

- **Superficial muscles**

- **Suprahyoid muscles** (above the hyoid bone)

- **Infrahyoid muscles** (below the hyoid bone)

The **hyoid bone** is a small, horseshoe-shaped bone tucked under your jaw. It's the only bone in the body not directly connected to any other bone—suspended by muscles like a **floating anchor**. The muscles above and below it move it like the rigging of a sailboat, shifting it up or down to help with actions like chewing, swallowing, and speaking.

- The muscles **below** the hyoid pull it downward and help anchor it to the throat and chest. These muscles let you **swallow food and return to breathing without missing a beat**.

- The muscles **above** the hyoid lift it upward and anchor it to the jaw and skull. These help you chew and separate your teeth.

The **superficial muscles** of the front of the neck are involved in facial expression and anchoring the jaw to the neck.

When you smile, you smile with more than just your face. Your neck **smiles too**. And when you move your head—up, down, or side to side—these muscles help make it happen.

Now, if you're reading this and thinking, *"But Jenn, I'm here for Spinal Intelligence, not an anatomy lecture,"* I get it.

Hang in there. The first part of Spinal Intelligence is the cultivated awareness of how your spine participates in every movement. Knowing what's under the hood, so to speak, can make it a lot easier to sense and feel when the spine moves.

BEFORE YOU MOVE ON, ASK YOURSELF:

》 Based on what you just learned about the front-of-neck muscles, what things might affect how well you move your head?

(You'll find some ideas at the end of the chapter.)

SIDE OF THE NECK:

The muscles on the sides of your neck connect the neck to the upper ribs.

If your ribs are anchored by your position, like you are lying on your back or in a variation of child's pose, these muscles move your neck.

If your torso is fixed, they help lift your first rib—**which plays a key role in breathing.**

BACK OF THE NECK:

The muscles in the back of the neck are also arranged in **three layers:**

- **Superficial** (closest to the skin)

- **Deep**

- **Deepest** (closest to the spine)

The deepest layers are like the **internal scaffolding** of your neck, supporting your head and vertebrae from the inside out.

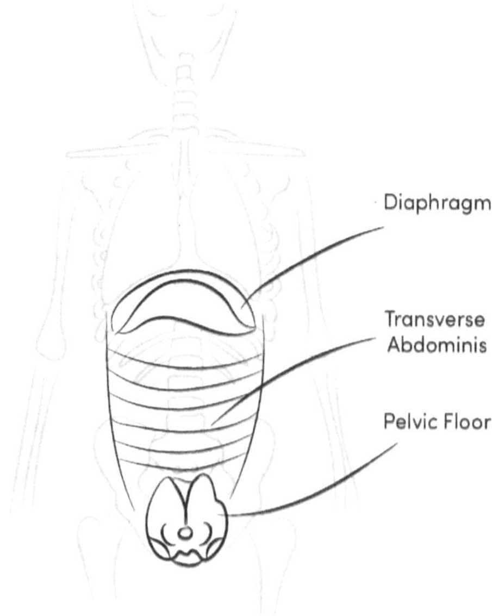

The more superficial layers connect the head to the torso and help with motions like shrugging your shoulders, turning your head, or tilting your ear toward your shoulder.

THE THORACIC SPINE:
LAYERS, RIBS, AND BREATHING

Let's move into the middle part of the spine—**the thoracic spine**.

There are usually **12 vertebrae** in this section (usually, because once in a while someone will have 13, like a little *vertebra bonus*). These vertebrae continue to increase in size as they move away from the head. They have **discs between them**, ligaments encasing them, and—importantly—**each thoracic vertebra has a pair of ribs attached to it.**

So if you have 12 thoracic vertebrae, you have 12 pairs of ribs.

Your **rib cage** protects your **vital organs**—and by vital, I mean the things that keep you alive, like your **heart** and **lungs**.

Your 12 pairs of ribs fall into three categories:

- **True ribs:** These attach directly to your breastbone (sternum).

- **False ribs:** These don't attach to the sternum itself, but instead to the cartilage of the sternum. *(Cartilage is strong, flexible connective tissue that lines joints and bones, acting like a shock absorber.)*

- **Floating ribs:** These don't connect to the front of the rib cage at all. Instead, they end within the abdominal muscles.

Because your **lungs** sit behind the rib cage and your **diaphragm** rests at its base, every time you breathe or move, the **ribs move too.**

Your breath is kind of like a **butterfly**—when you inhale, it flutters down your throat into your lungs, expanding your diaphragm and rib cage, and ripples out through the rest of your body.

When you exhale, the breath reverses its butterfly effect: the diaphragm moves up, the ribs draw inward, the pressure in the lungs shifts so they deflate like a balloon, and the breath flutters up and out.

MUSCLES OF THE THORACIC REGION

There are several muscles in this part of the spine. Deep muscles run along each side of the spinal column, from **head to pelvis,** anchoring the spine to itself and offering **stability and structure.**

At this point, the **muscular layers become interwoven**, not as clearly separated as in the neck. So rather than break down every single muscle, I'll give you a **brief overview** of what some of these layers do.

Your **shoulder blade** (scapula) glides along the back of your rib cage.

Between the shoulder blade and the rib cage is a muscle that looks like a **serrated knife**—appropriately named the **serratus anterior**. ("Serratus" is Latin for "saw-like"—anatomists were pretty clever with their naming.)

The shoulder blade acts as an **anchor for your arm**. And because your arm can make a lot of different movements, it probably won't surprise you that **17 muscles** attach the arm to the shoulder blade.

THAT MEANS:

If you reach your arm overhead right now, a **whole group of muscles** along the back of your rib cage are at work just to help you lift your arm. These layers of muscle build up between your **spine** and your **skin**, like a living, dynamic support system.

BREATHING MUSCLES AND THE CLAVICLE

Between each rib are muscles called the **intercostals**, which help expand and contract the rib cage as you breathe.

(So remember: **the rib cage moves when you breathe**—and the intercostals make that possible.)

At the top of the rib cage is the **collarbone** (clavicle). Think of it as the **top front of the "arm ring"**. It connects your breastbone to your shoulder blade. The joint where the clavicle meets the shoulder blade plays a **pivotal role in letting your arm reach overhead.**

Several important muscles attach to the clavicle, including:

- **Your chest muscles (pectorals)**

- **Your trapezius**—one of the large, superficial muscles of your mid-back.

These muscles are involved in **breathing, anchoring the arm, and moving the shoulders and arms.**

THE XIPHOID PROCESS
AND THE CORE

At the bottom of your breastbone is a small, **dagger-shaped bone** called the **xiphoid process.**

The word *xiphoid* comes from the Greek word *xiphos,* meaning "little dagger."

This little dagger is **a key anchor point** for several muscles in your torso:

- On the **backside,** the **diaphragm** attaches here.

- On the **front side,** several **abdominal muscles** attach, including:
  - **Transverse abdominis**
  - **Rectus abdominis**
  - **Internal and external obliques**

These are the muscles you likely associate with your **core.**

ANOTHER MOMENT OF REFLECTION:

» Based on what you just learned, what might the interplay between the xiphoid process and your abdominal muscles mean for "Spinal Intelligence"?

(I haven't defined that term yet–but I will soon, I promise!)

LAYER UPON LAYER

Phew. That's a lot—but can you start to see how many layers exist between your skin and your spine?

In between many of those layers—and surrounding your muscles—is a connective tissue called **fascia**.

Fascia looks a bit like **saran wrap**: thin, stretchy, and strong. It serves multiple functions:

- Provides **support and stability**

- Connects **muscles to bones** and to other structures

- **Transmits forces** during movement

If your back were made up of a **thick quilt**, with **interwoven layers** and a **thin sheath** separating each section, that's what the muscles and fascia of your back are like.

The quilt can stretch to fit different movements but always returns to its original shape—**unless one part gets twisted, bunched, or stuck.**

** To be clear, whether or not your fascia gets twisted, bunched, or stuck remains up for debate. These are the words people often used to describe the sensation that occurs when they aren't able to twist, bend, or move easily.*

A QUICK NOTE ON MOVEMENT AND VIBRATION

Before we move on to the **lumbar spine**, it's worth mentioning this:

When you move, your muscles generate tension. Tension occurs when something stretches. That tension creates pressure within the body, and pressure is information for your nervous system.

All movement requires interaction with force. In physics, force refers to an action that changes or maintains motion, or that influences the shape of the body. Gravity is the constant backdrop for every movement we make. If I were to do a forward roll right now, my motor cortex would organize the sequence, my muscles would generate the tension needed to create that coordination, the ground would support me, and gravity would help carry me through space. The way these forces meet and exchange energy shapes the experience of the movement.

Some movements ask for a greater exchange than others, generating more acceleration, more pressure into the ground, and more momentum moving through you. A forward roll is one example of this amplified interaction.

When I say that "forces are transmitted through the fascia," this is what I'm referring to—but it's deeper than just the gross movement.

At the level of the **cell**, there is always movement happening via **vibration**.

The fancy word for this is **mechanotransduction**—it refers to how **cells communicate** through mechanical signals like pressure and vibration.

So every time you move, there's a **cascade of vibrations** happening within you. As long as you're alive, you are **vibrating**, on some level, all the time.

THE LUMBAR SPINE: YOUR FOUNDATION FOR LOAD BEARING

At the very bottom of your spine sits the lumbar spine. These vertebra are the largest and thickest of the bunch, built to bear serious weight. Like the thoracic vertebra above them, they have thick intervertebral discs and strong ligaments that give the lower back both structure and stability.

The lumbar vertebra connect your rib cage to your pelvis, forming a sturdy bridge between the upper and lower body. They're designed to handle big loads—like when you lift something heavy or carry a backpack.

If I do a handstand, my body weight travels down my spine into my arms. Since I'm upside down, there's actually less load on my lumbar spine than when I'm standing.

But if I do a shoulder press, the weight from my arms travels down into my spine, loading it more directly. That's why a shoulder press is more effective for loading the lumbar spine than a handstand. Neither is "better"—they simply challenge the spine in different ways.

THE FRONT OF THE LUMBAR SPINE: ORGANS, MUSCLES, AND FASCIA

In front of the lumbar spine sits a thin protective layer called the peritoneum, which holds several key organs. Layered over that are the abdominal wall muscles you've met before—the transverse abdominis, internal obliques, and external obliques—stretching from your ribs to your pelvis.

Fascia, the body's connective tissue, weaves between these muscle layers. It ties the front of your torso to the sides and back, creating a wraparound support system.

THE SIDE OF THE LUMBAR SPINE: A 3D LAYERED QUILT

If you shift your attention to the sides of your torso, you'll find muscles linking the middle back and torso to the pelvis. Closest to the spine are deep, vertical muscles. On top of those are more diagonally arranged muscles—imagine that "quilt" analogy from earlier, but wrapped into a cylinder, with some patches stitched on the bias. This arrangement gives the torso strength, flexibility, and the ability to move in many directions.

THE BACK OF THE LUMBAR SPINE: DEEP AND SUPERFICIAL CONNECTIONS

The side layers blend into the muscles at the back. Some of these deep muscles run the entire length of the spine, while others continue down from the thoracic spine, linking the shoulder blades to the pelvis. Still others connect the back of the lumbar spine to the front of the pelvis—another way the spine anchors to the lower body.

THE LUMBAR TAPESTRY: FULL-TORSO SUPPORT

All of these layers form a single, integrated support network. The latissimus dorsi and thoracolumbar fascia connect the upper body to the pelvis. The quadratus lumborum and obliques provide cylindrical support along the sides. The tendons of the obliques and transverse abdominis wrap around and enclose the rectus abdominis, creating a corset-like stability that keeps you upright.

YOUR ARMS AND PELVIS NEED THIS CONNECTION

This lumbar "tapestry" forms the home base for your arms and pelvis. Without it, those structures would be floating in space, disconnected from your center. This is why strong, functional lumbar muscles are so important—not just for posture, but for every movement you make.

WHY "CORE TRAINING" IS A MISNOMER

Now that you've seen how interconnected the lumbar region is, it's easy to see why "isolating" the core is tricky. Finding the exact center of any muscle group here would require peeling away layer after layer—and even then, you'd still be affecting neighboring tissues.

That's why the idea of training one tiny, specific spot is misleading. You can bias certain muscles, yes, but others will always be involved. In reality, everything you do is core training—whether you realize it or not.

WHAT'S NEXT: DEFINING SPINAL INTELLIGENCE

That's the structural side of the story. But the spine isn't just a stack of bones and muscles—it's a living, sensing, responsive system. Before we explore the mind-body connection, it's time to answer the big question: what exactly is spinal intelligence?

I offered a definition earlier, but let's dive into the meaning a little more. The word spinal refers to the spine, the very structure I've been waxing poetic about for the last 3,000 words. It's your center, the core of your physical being, and, as you'll learn in the next chapter, a major hub for processing the information you receive from the world and determining how you respond to it.

Intelligence is a funny word. According to Merriam-Webster, it is "the ability to learn, to understand, and to apply knowledge to manipulate one's environment." To have spinal intelligence might sound like the spine is a separate entity with its own mind—which isn't exactly how movement works. But you—your whole self, mind and body—can develop a deep awareness and understanding of how your spine supports you and participates in movement. You can learn its structure and, more importantly, sense different aspects of your spine when you choose to.

This simple act of awareness has a variety of benefits. Sensing different aspects of yourself creates a clearer picture, or "map," of you in your brain. While it won't help you land a new job, buy a house, run faster, or carve a six-pack, it will increase your confidence, help you feel calmer, and improve your overall body awareness.

I like to say, movement creates more movement. I've used the concepts in this book with hundreds of clients and students: helping people gain confidence in their balance, guiding individuals toward stronger push-ups, supporting people as they lift heavier weights, and even assisting others in finding more comfort in a handstand. I've applied these principles in yoga studios, pole and aerial studios, and CrossFit boxes.

The principles of Spinal Intelligence will help you feel more connected, more aware, and more confident in your ability to adjust when things aren't working—and to trust the resilience of your structure. Whether you've just finished rehabbing an injury and want to return to your activities, you're looking to maximize body awareness for a specific sport, or you simply want to feel more integrated throughout your day, Spinal Intelligence offers an entry point—a way to experience a mind-body connection.

I'm continually amazed by a person's capacity to learn and change. This capacity stays with us, regardless of age or physical ability, until our very last day. When I was preparing to start graduate school, I told a client I felt "too old" to be getting a master's degree. She looked at me and said, "Two years will pass whether you go to graduate school or not." In that instant, I realized I wouldn't regret spending the next two years deepening my knowledge. Learning is always a choice.

That moment changed the way I approached teaching movement. I stopped seeing it as a single moment in time meant solely to improve physical health, and started seeing it as an opportunity to give people something they could carry forward. Yes, there were physical benefits, but there was also something deeper: awareness. Awareness that gave them autonomy, resilience, and the ability to trust their bodies' capacity to withstand stress and, in some cases, to heal.

Your ability to learn new movements, master new skills, and adapt—to get stronger, more flexible, more coordinated—is truly awe-inspiring.

Before you move on, pause and think of a moment in the past three months when your physical strength surprised you. Maybe you helped a friend lift something heavy, hoisted your 90-pound dog into the car, or sprinted up a hill. Whatever it was, write it down. Take a moment to be grateful for it.

Because now, we're going to explore the next layer—the way your spine talks to your brain, your brain talks to your body, and how this constant conversation shapes every movement you make. Get ready: we're about to dive into text neck and the nervous system, where science meets sensation, and where your awareness will start to transform how you move.

CHAPTER 1 REFLECTIONS:

Earlier, I asked a few questions that I promised to answer at the end of the chapter. Let's start with the first:

What things might affect how well you move your neck?

Here's a short (but not exhaustive) list. As you'll learn in later chapters, the interconnectedness of your senses means that something far away in your body could influence what's happening at your head. Some possibilities include:

- Where you're looking

- How you use your jaw

- How you use your arms

- How you use your ears

How can the arms affect what's happening at the spine?

The muscles of the arms are intertwined with the muscles of the back. Your ability to move your arms in different ways–and your baseline arm strength–can influence how connected you feel in your spine. (We'll explore this in more detail later.)

What might the interplay between the xiphoid process and your abdominal muscles mean for "Spinal Intelligence"?

The position of the xiphoid process changes the length and tension in the abdominal muscles. You can use this relationship to deepen a sensation of work, increase a feeling of stretch, or facilitate greater connection through specific parts of the spine.

Which parts of your body will affect the muscles in your core?

All of them–which is why a good coach can cue something seemingly unrelated, and you'll feel your core light up like a Christmas tree.

CHAPTER 2:
THE NECK: MORE THAN JUST POSTURE

Jean (not her real name), a client I see occasionally, was standing in front of me, concerned. She's tall, 5'9", and spends a lot of time on her phone.

"Why do you think you have text neck?"

"Because my neck hurts and my head is forward a lot."

It makes sense she'd connect the two. She's educated, follows popular fitness and wellness influencers on Instagram and TikTok, and is proactive when it comes to fixing what she sees as dysfunctions.

But here's the thing: despite what social media and even major outlets like *The New York Times* say about texting and technology causing neck pain, the research just doesn't back it up.

That doesn't mean neck pain isn't real—it absolutely is. And the good news? If you do a routine that combines strengthening, body awareness, and stretching, muscular neck pain often improves.

I didn't explain all of this to her in the moment. Instead, I showed her how to feel where her head was in space, adding drills that had her look toward something specific. I also included whole-body strengthening exercises, because the neck doesn't exist in isolation.

We *want* posture to be the culprit. It feels logical—if someone's head is always hanging forward, surely that must be a problem, right?

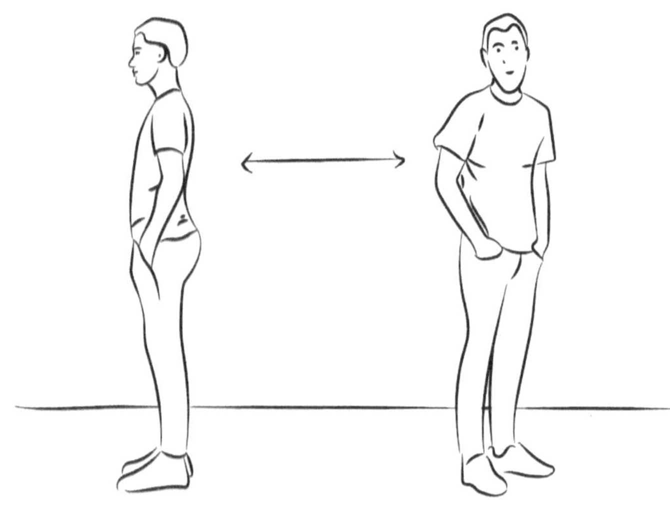

Let's look at Stephen Nedoroscik, the Olympic gymnast. In almost every photo online, his head appears to be thrusting forward. It would be easy to assume he's a textbook case of "text neck" (no pun intended).

But if you watched the 2024 Olympics, you might remember him as "the pommel horse guy." His routine helped the U.S. men's gymnastics team take home the bronze, and he picked up his own bronze medal on pommel horse.

Nedoroscik lives with two eye conditions—one that causes his eyes to cross and point in different directions, and another that makes him sensitive to light. Since your eyes are literally connected to your head, vision can influence how you hold it (more on that in a bit).

He also has asthma, which affects his breathing. And how you breathe plays a role in how you position your head, since the lungs and breathing muscles sit right below the neck.

So it's not surprising that Nedoroscik is often photographed with his head in a forward position. But here's the thing: he doesn't have neck pain. Other than a hand fracture and a couple of elbow issues, he's been remarkably injury-free despite the fact that his sport requires throwing his body around a horizontal, stationary object that is 3.77 feet off the floor.

POSTURE AS A TEMPORARY POSITION

It's tricky to reconcile the idea that a person's posture—a temporary position they're in before moving to the next one—isn't definitively linked to, well, anything.

WHY "TEXT NECK" ISN'T REAL

Which is why "text neck" isn't a real thing. It's just the posture required to text, usually broken up by other activities (unless someone is texting 40 hours a week). Neck pain, on the other hand, is influenced by a variety of factors. Posture isn't permanent; it's simply a pause before you transition into something else. You are dynamic, which means you are always moving.

WHY POSTURE-FOCUSED PROGRAMS HELP

So why do some people feel so much better after a physical therapy program, Pilates sessions, or personal training that emphasizes posture?

The answer, much like the human body itself, is multi-factorial. But from a purely physical standpoint, the benefits often come down to two things: a) putting your body in different positions, and b) getting stronger.

And then there's the human side of it. People like support. We're social creatures, and simply having another person guide you, encourage you, and help you pay attention to your body can make you feel better.

POSTURE IN EVERYDAY LIFE

Take Stephen Nedoroscik. He's strong—strong enough to support his body in a variety of positions, including one where his neck looks a little more forward.

Unless your profession requires you to stay in an awkward position for long periods of time with minimal shifting, like a jeweler, seamstress, or dentist, most of us don't hold one position long enough for it to be a problem. But if you are forced to stay in one spot, that prolonged posture can become an issue. In fact, dentists, jewelers, and sewing machine operators all show notably high rates of neck pain compared to the general population.

PROLONGED POSTURES AND OVERUSE

You can think of prolonged, awkward positions as an opportunity for an overuse injury. Overuse injuries happen when the stress of a load exceeds your ability to counter it through muscular effort. So if you're bent over a patient's mouth for eight hours a day, using tiny instruments, and adding in all the other stresses of life, the risk of neck pain goes up.

But here's the thing—not all dentists (or jewelers, or sewing machine operators) end up with neck pain. Just like not all athletes develop overuse injuries.

THE BIG QUESTION

Which, of course, leads to the next logical question (and I do love logic): why do some people develop pain and others don't?

THE NERVOUS SYSTEM:
BRAIN AND BODY INTERTWINED

You take in a lot of inputs throughout the day. Some are welcome, like a warm bath or a massage.

Except—not everyone likes baths or massages. Which means not everyone responds the same way to the same input.

Maybe you've heard of the nervous system: the network in your body that lets you think, move, sense the world, and regulate basic functions. Nerves carry electrical signals to and from your brain and spinal cord about all kinds of things—temperature, smell, pressure, even your overall energy levels.

You can think of the nervous system as the system that collects information and signals how to respond. But it's not just raw data—it's filtered through your perception.

PERCEPTION SHAPES RESPONSE

Back to the bath example. Imagine you love warm water—the way it surrounds you, how it warms you on a cold day. Just the thought of sliding into a tub filled with salts or bubbles makes you relax. You can feel your muscles softening as you picture it.

Now flip it. Imagine baths feel claustrophobic. You don't like sitting in a tub for a long time. Maybe you're thinking about bacteria unless it's freshly scrubbed. And the heat? Miserable. You hate being hot.

In that scenario, a bath isn't soothing at all. If anything, being forced into one would make you anxious—amped up, squirmy, definitely not relaxed.

Our perception shapes how we respond. It's built on our history, our likes and dislikes, and how we're feeling in this particular moment.

It's also influenced by basics like how much sleep we're getting and how well we're managing the stressors of daily life.

STRESS, SHIELDS, AND PROLONGED POSITIONS

What does all of this have to do with someone's ability to tolerate prolonged, awkward positions? Let's imagine two dentists: James and Adam.

TWO DENTISTS, TWO STORIES

James and Adam are both 48. They've been practicing dentistry since they were 28, so each has 20 years of experience. Both graduated near the top of their class, and both are considered excellent at what they do.

James's story: James has an active life outside of work. He loves dentistry, but he also loves mountain biking and spending time with his long-term partner. He values work-life balance and regularly takes vacations where he and his partner hike and bike in different parts of the world. James lifts weights once or twice a week to stay strong, drinks alcohol occasionally, and uses THC gummies fairly regularly to help with sleep. Sleep is a struggle—he often gets no more than five solid hours a night. Recently, his mother passed away, which left him grieving and in a mild depression for about six months.

Adam's story: Adam is a divorced father of two. He spends a lot of time with his kids, often at their sporting events and dance competitions. He worries about money (the divorce was expensive), so he takes on more patients than he'd like to stay afloat. He works long hours and doesn't love his job, though being good at it gives him a sense of satisfaction. Adam doesn't have time to exercise, but he does have a regular meditation practice, which helps him sleep. He averages eight hours of sleep per night and avoids alcohol and THC. Recently, he joined a men's group to rebuild his social life.

INSULTS AND SHIELDS

Both James and Adam have factors in their lives that can reduce their tolerance for prolonged positions. You can think of these factors as **insults**. The more insults, the lower someone's ability to tolerate stress.

- **James's insults:** 3 → difficulty sleeping, grief from losing his mom, and mild, persistent depression.

- **Adam's insults:** 2 → financial stress and anxiety, and lack of exercise.

But they also have protective factors. Let's call these **shields**—the things that buffer stress. Shields might include an active social life, a supportive family, work-life balance, regular vacations, meditation, exercise, hobbies, or learning something new.

- **James's shields:** 4 ↠ a supportive relationship, work-life balance, a hobby he loves, and regular exercise.

- **Adam's shields:** 4 ↠ a strong commitment to his kids, meditation practice, prioritizing sleep, and his new men's group.

STRESS IS PERSONAL

We'll return to James and Adam a little later, but something to keep in mind as you think about shields and insults is this:

what you see as stress might not be stressful to me, and vice versa.

I'm time-sensitive. Just the thought of procrastinating—whether it's paying bills or finishing a project—stresses me out. And yet procrastination has been linked to creativity, so it's not without benefits. For me, though, the anxiety outweighs the creative upside.

On the other hand, I know people who *thrive* on procrastination. The closer the deadline, the more energized they feel, and the better they perform. For them, procrastination isn't a bad stress—it's a good stress.

WHEN STRESS FEELS GOOD

Conversely, when I go for a six-mile run before work in the morning, I don't perceive it as stress, even though physically, running places real stress on my heart and lungs. I find my morning runs relaxing: a chance to be by myself outside, an opportunity to get lost in my thoughts, and a moment to outline chapters of this book.

Other people, however, have a viscerally negative reaction to the thought of running six miles. They may not enjoy running or aren't physically prepared to cover more than a few steps. For them, the idea of being forced to run six miles sparks real concern about potential injury, soreness, or significant discomfort. Running six miles is a fantastic stress for me, but for others, it's a potentially injurious one.

STRESS, STRAIN, AND ADAPTATION

The perception of whether something is stressful comes down to the balance between stress, strain, and adaptation. All stress is an insult, even the "good" kind. **Strain**, in the physical sense, is how your body responds—muscles deform under load, accommodating the stress placed on them.

Your body also has a natural mechanism for resilience: **adaptation**. Strain creates inflammation in the muscles, which triggers a cascade of healing responses. Over time, the tissue becomes stronger and more resistant to future stress.

In a psychological sense, strain refers to the negative consequences of stress. How you respond determines whether the outcome is **adaptive**, like mental resistance training, or **maladaptive**, like pulling a muscle.

Whether your response is adaptive or maladaptive depends on:

- How much control you feel over the situation

- Your past responses to similar stressors

- The tools you have to handle the stress in its current form

CHRONIC STRESS AND NECK PAIN

Chronic neck pain doesn't appear overnight—it creeps in slowly and almost imperceptibly.

Chronic stress behaves the same way: one insult followed by another, creating a series of maladaptive strains over time.

SPINAL INTELLIGENCE:
THE MIND-BODY CONNECTION

You might be wondering how this relates to spinal intelligence. Remember that part of intelligence is confidence. How confident are you that you can respond to the perceived stress in an adaptive way?

That's the way it relates on a psychological level. On a physiological level, your spine is a hub of activity. The nerves that carry information about the world, your internal state, and your physical responses exit your vertebrae like roots of a tree. They spread throughout your body, communicating via electrical impulses that send information along nerves back to your central nervous system—your brain and spinal cord.

Think of your spine as an information superhighway. This unavoidable connection between mind and body is one of your greatest strengths for feeling balanced and connected.

POTENTIAL INSULTS TO WATCH

When the central nervous system decides specific stressors in life are threatening, your physical response mirrors that, whether the stressors are physical, emotional, social, or lifestyle-related. These stressors act as "insults" that can accumulate over time. Being aware of them helps you understand what might be tipping you out of balance. This gives you the opportunity to assess and determine where adaptation is needed.

EXAMPLES OF STRESSORS INCLUDE:

Physical Stressors:

- Lack of physical exercise

- Trouble sleeping

- Untreated allergies

- Acute injury (like stubbing a toe or twisting an ankle)

Emotional / Psychological Stressors:

- Negative work stress

- Negative family stress

- Feelings of loneliness

- Feelings of depression

- Feelings of anxiety

Social / Life Stressors:

- Lack of social support

- Divorce

- Caregiving duties (for a child, parent, spouse, or family member)

Lifestyle / Nutritional Stressors:

- A nutrient-deficient diet

- Regular alcohol consumption (more than one drink, three times a week)

POTENTIAL SHIELDS TO BUILD

Shields are protective factors that help buffer stress and support your physical and mental well-being. Being aware of them helps you identify what's already working and what you could add to improve your resilience.

EXAMPLES INCLUDE:

Social / Relationship Shields:

- A sense of community

- A fulfilling family life

- A partner or spouse

Physical Activity Shields:

- Regular cardiovascular activity

- Regular resistance training

- A fulfilling hobby

Mental / Emotional Shields:

- A sense of purpose

- A regular meditation practice

- Consistent sleep (for most people, 7–8.5 hours per night)

- Regularly learning new things

- A creative outlet

Lifestyle / Nutritional Shields:

- Regularly consuming whole foods

- Regular time in nature

- Financial security

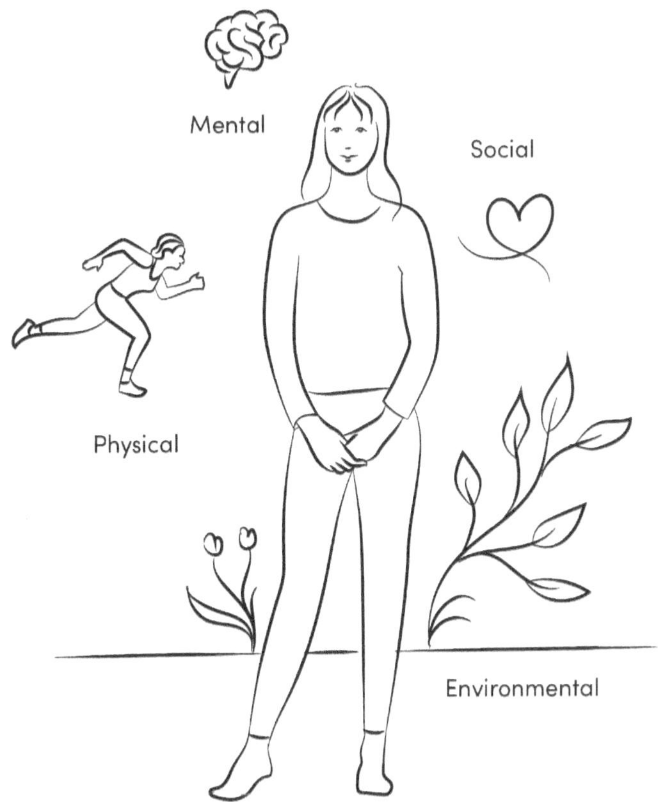

YOUR NERVOUS SYSTEM AND STRESS

The part of your nervous system that revs up in response to stress can make you feel antsy, nervous, or anxious—but it can also make you feel energized, excited, or ready for whatever you are doing.

How you respond is partially determined by how prepared you are. For example, I am ready to run six miles, so the thought of running six miles feels fun rather than daunting. It's also partially determined by your relationship to the task at hand. On days when it's windy or icy, the run that I generally look forward to becomes a daunting task to get through. My relationship to the task is context dependent.

SHIELDS, INSULTS, AND THRESHOLDS

Back to James and Adam. Are positive factors/shields enough to offset the physical stress required by someone's job?

It might be for James, who spends less time working than Adam, meaning he spends less time in prolonged, awkward positions. Or it might not. Everyone has a different threshold for insults. Adam's threshold might be higher; he may be able to work at the edge of his limit because of his meditation practice without tipping over into strain.

There is a fine line between **enough stress** to keep life interesting (and your body strong) and **too much stress,** which leaves you feeling exhausted, unfocused, or physically unable to handle daily demands.

What helps?

- Physical strength

- Social support

- Curiosity and learning

- Breathing or meditation practices

Life happens. We all go through periods with more insults than we would like. The balance you maintain during calmer times—between shields and insults—builds your resilience, so you can withstand an onslaught of challenges without falling apart.

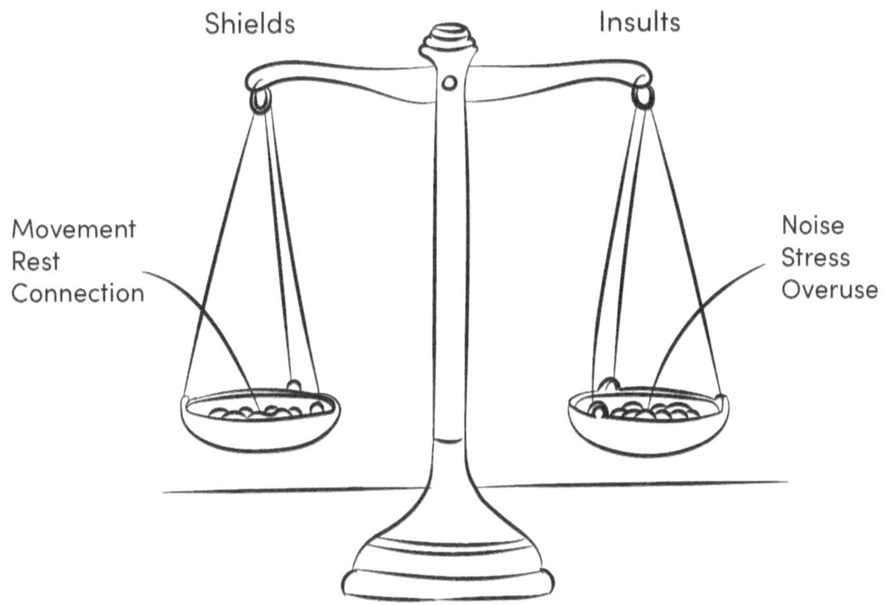

MIND-BODY CONNECTION

The mind and the body are like the underlying design on a quilt. They are intertwined, influencing how the layers fold, stretch, and rest on each other. If you influence the mind, you influence the body—and if you influence the body, you influence the mind.

BUILD YOUR RESILIENCE:
INSULTS & SHIELDS WORKSHEET

STEP 1: CHECK YOUR BOXES

Potential Insults (Stressors)	Potential Shields (Protective Factors)
☐ Lack of physical exercise	☐ A sense of community
☐ Trouble sleeping	☐ A fulfilling family life
☐ Untreated allergies	☐ A partner or spouse
☐ Moving	☐ Regular cardiovascular activity
☐ Negative work stress	☐ Regular resistance training

Potential Insults (Stressors)	Potential Shields (Protective Factors)
☐ Negative family stress	☐ A fulfilling hobby
☐ Feelings of loneliness	☐ A sense of purpose
☐ Feelings of depression	☐ A regular meditation practice
☐ Feelings of anxiety	☐ Consistent sleep (7-8.5 hrs/night)
☐ Lack of social support	☐ Regularly learning new things
☐ Divorce	☐ Regularly consuming whole foods
☐ Caregiving duties	☐ A creative outlet
☐ A nutrient-deficient diet	☐ Regular time in nature
☐ Regular alcohol consumption	☐ Financial security

Tip: Use a pencil or pen to check off items that apply to you.

STEP 2: **REFLECT**

- Which insults could you reduce or manage better?

- Which shields could be strengthened or added?

Write a few notes here:

____

____

____

____

____

____

____

____

Today	Next Week	Next Month

STEP 4: **READ ALOUD & ADJUST**

- Say your plan out loud.

- How do you feel?

- Are your goals realistic and achievable?

At the beginning of the chapter, I mentioned my client, Jean, and her "text neck." Jean sees a physical therapist regularly. The physical therapist assured her that there was nothing serious going on (and was more than likely the one who told her she had text neck).

My role with Jean was to provide support. I did this through a multi-faceted approach that included **body awareness, general strength, and instilling confidence,** reassuring her that she wasn't going to damage her neck by looking at her phone.

Now let's juxtapose that with another client of mine I will call Brie. Brie is roughly the same age as Jean (late 30s), but she had the opposite problem— **military neck**.

Brie was born without a **left sternocleidomastoid (SCM)**. The SCM is the muscle in the front of the neck that connects the back of the head to the breastbone and collarbone. It's important for anchoring the head and torso to each other while allowing the head to rotate.

Anatomy books show the muscles most people have, but there are always outliers. Since humans are extremely adaptable, missing a muscle usually isn't a big deal—other muscles pick up the slack, so to speak, and most people don't even realize a muscle is missing. Nobody checks inside when you are born to make sure you have every single muscle anatomists have identified.

Brie teaches fitness and is acutely aware of her posture and her missing SCM. She consciously keeps her head pulled back. She's also very good at maintaining shields, prioritizing supportive habits in her life.

Unlike Jean, who needed strength and reassurance, Brie needed to **trust that relaxing her neck wouldn't hurt her.** Constantly holding her head in one position was creating tension.

And the tension was creating discomfort.

So we worked on building up the trust that she could relax her neck. I gave her **breathing drills that doubled as neck stretches,** building her confidence to let her head hang in different positions. I continued to provide support, helping bolster her confidence so that she could ultimately trust her body to do something she had previously avoided at all costs.

I used movement interventions with both my text neck client and my military neck client that address more than just the neck. I'm not a medical professional, but I understand movement. That means I can **leave the neck alone** and work on developing flexibility and strength in other areas that influence the neck's position. I also use **body awareness exercises** that don't add stress or load to the neck but help someone sense where their head is in space.

Spinal intelligence isn't about treating pain; it's about helping you feel more confident in what you can do. A byproduct of building confidence is you get tools to manage the vague muscular aches and pains that don't have a specific cause.

Based on what you have learned about the neck, can you think of **three exercises, movements, or body awareness drills** that might help Jean, the client who thinks she has text neck?

Based on what you have learned about the neck, can you think of three exercises, movements, or body awareness drills that might help Brie, the client with a lot of neck tension?

I will share some ideas and real-life examples of exercises I used with them in a minute, but before I do, here are some of the main concepts from this chapter. Take a moment to read them over, reflect on what resonates with you, and think about how you can apply this information in your own movement practice.

THREE EXERCISES FOR JEAN (WHO THOUGHT HER NECK PAIN WAS LINKED TO FORWARD HEAD POSTURE)

1. **Seated Head Reach (Body Awareness)**

   - Sit and feel your sitting bones (the bony knobs at the bottom of your pelvis).

   - Reach your head away from your sitting bones. Hold for a count of three, then relax.

   - Repeat 4–6 times, imagining your head reaching further away from your sitting bones each time.

2. **Lean and Pull (Strength & Motor Control)**

   - Hold onto gymnastics rings, a suspension trainer, a counter, or stall bars.

   - Lean back, imagining a line running from the center of your head all the way down to where your feet meet the floor.

   - Organize your body along that line.

   - Pull your body toward the support, hold for a count of three, then lower yourself down.

   - Make sure you are breathing the entire time.

3. **Weighted Side-to-Side Reach (Flexibility, Body Awareness, & Coordination)**

   - Stand with your feet wide. Shift your weight to the right as you reach your right hand toward the wall.

   - Watch your right hand the entire time.

   - Then reach your hand up toward the ceiling and to the left.

   - Go back and forth between these two positions, breathing steadily throughout.

THREE EXERCISES FOR BRIE
(WHO HAS TENSION FROM KEEPING HER HEAD BACK)

1. **Hands-and-Knees Stretch (Flexibility & Relaxation)**

   - Come into a hands-and-knees position.

   - Shift your hips back slightly and push the back of your shirt toward the ceiling, letting your head hang down.

   - Take three breaths, using the inhale to expand the back and the exhale to relax your jaw.

2. **Push-Up Flow (Body Awareness & Motor Control)**

   - Come into a straight-arm push-up position with your knees off the floor.

   - Push the hips back, letting your head hang loosely.

   - Reach the hips forward, letting the spine round as you move back into a push-up position.

   - Allow the head to move last.

3. **Arm Rotation Flow (Flexibility, Internal Strength, & Motor Control)**

   - Stand and extend your right arm straight out to the side.

   - Rotate the back of your right hand down toward the floor as you reach the arm long. Your right shoulder will rotate forward, and your middle back will round.

   - Once you can't rotate any more, bring the arm across the body, brushing the back of the hand behind your head from the left side, then extend it back out to the right.

QUICK REFERENCE: NECK EXERCISES

For Jean (forward head posture concern)

- **Awareness through length** → Sit tall, feel sitting bones, gently reach head upward. Hold 3 sec, repeat 4–6x.

- **Organize around a line** → Lean back holding rings/counter, imagine head-to-feet line, pull in, hold 3 sec, lower.

- **Reaching with awareness** → Feet wide, shift right, reach right hand sideways/up/across, follow with eyes, repeat.

For Brie (neck tension from pulling head back)

- **Breathing into the back** → On hands/knees, hips back, head heavy, breathe into back ribs, soften jaw.

- **Spinal wave in plank** → From push-up, hips back/head loose → round spine forward into plank, head moves last.

- **Arm spiral with rotation** → Arm out to side, rotate hand down/shoulder forward, sweep arm across body and behind head, extend again.

Use as a quick refresher before teaching or practicing.

CHAPTER 3:
WHEN STRENGTH CHANGES EVERYTHING

—

A CONVERSATION WITH MEGAN

I was chatting with a client I see occasionally—let's call her Megan. Megan is a high-level pole dancer and pole dance teacher who had spinal surgery last year. After surgery, she went to physical therapy, but the therapists weren't familiar with the physical demands of pole dancing. When her sessions ended, she didn't feel adequately prepared to return to dancing and teaching without risking reinjury.

I'm a low-level pole dancer myself, but I love movement and understand the physical skills, strength, and flexibility required for what she does. That shared language helped us work together effectively.

A SHOULDER FIX–AND AN UNEXPECTED BENEFIT

During one of our sessions, Megan mentioned she was experiencing shoulder pain. I showed her two simple exercises and suggested she do them regularly.

When we caught up recently, she told me that not only had her shoulder pain disappeared, but her chronic neck pain—something she'd dealt with for years—had also become almost non-existent since starting those two shoulder exercises.

This is one of the unintended benefits of developing general, total-body strength.

HOW THE SHOULDER AND NECK WORK TOGETHER

As you learned in Chapter One, the body is deeply interconnected. The shoulder muscles attach to the collarbone in the front and the scapula in the back. The neck muscles anchor the head to the torso through those same structures—the clavicle in front and the scapula in back.

You can probably see where this is going: strengthening the shoulder muscles has a direct influence on the neck. Improving strength or stability in one region often brings unexpected relief in another.

AFTER SURGERY:
WHEN FLEXIBILITY CHANGES

Megan can perform advanced pole tricks. Before her spinal surgery, she had an incredibly bendy back and could drop into the splits with little to no warm-up.

Her back is still flexible compared to mine, but not as much as before. She can no longer slide into the splits easily, and even with a warm-up, she doesn't quite reach the flat splits she once had.

This isn't unusual after surgery. Much of your flexibility depends on what your nervous system perceives as safe. As mentioned in Chapter Two, your central nervous system (CNS), is the conductor that orchestrates how you move. Remember that it's made up of your brain and spinal cord. As a result, it's constantly receiving information from your peripheral nervous system (PNS), which includes all the nerves branching out from your spine. (I know, I know. You learned this already, but sometimes hearing something multiple times in different contexts makes it stick.)

When that input is altered—say, by a surgeon making an incision to remove part of a herniated disc—the CNS registers that change. The pressure from the disc on the nerve may decrease, but the tissue around the surgical site has also been disturbed. The skin, fascia, and muscle now send new signals.

THE NERVOUS SYSTEM'S
SMART RESPONSE

In back surgery, both the removal of a small piece of the disc and the incision itself create significant changes in input for the nervous system. The body's initial response during healing is tightness. This is a smart protective strategy. After all, moving too much and tearing healing tissue would be a bad idea.

But once the tissue has healed, that sense of tightness can linger. Gradual exposure to previously restricted positions can help the nervous system recognize those movements as safe again.

Imagine you are an aficionado of classical music and the oboe player of your favorite orchestra is out of commission. Rather than replace the oboe player, the orchestra is operating without an oboe player. You don't notice the oboe is missing some of the time, but for some pieces, the oboe provides a richness to the score that is noticeably absent.

Over time, the "conductor" begins to reintegrate the oboe player and the music sounds finished. You don't notice right away, but one day after a performance you realize the richness the music had been missing has returned.

The CNS works a lot like this after surgery. Initially, movement is restricted. As the area heals, you begin moving a little bit more and you begin to expose yourself to positions that were previously off limits. Through this gradual exposure, you begin to move more fully and your CNS allows smoother, more coordinated movement.

FINDING FLEXIBILITY AGAIN

Not everyone wants to do the splits after back surgery, but for those who do, it's absolutely possible, but you might need a different approach than before.

In Megan's case, she had relied heavily on her back to achieve many of her flexible positions. That strategy worked beautifully—until it didn't. And, as you'll see later in this chapter, that's a common pattern in how the body adapts and eventually calls for change.

HOW MUCH STRENGTH IS ENOUGH?

Back to this strength thing. A little bit of general strength goes a long way, but how much does a person really need?

Megan is strong enough to lift and hold her body upside down while hanging from a vertical metal pole. That's an impressive, highly specific kind of strength. But developing more general strength provides something different—strength that reinforces the muscular anchors of the neck, shoulders, torso, and legs.

For Megan, strengthening the muscles in her shoulders and mid-back created a stronger anchor for her head. Strong anchors give the central nervous system better information about where each body part is in space. This input functions like an internal compass: when the compass is working well, the nervous system can coordinate your next move with precision. When that compass is foggy or when your sense of "north, south, east, and west" isn't clear, the nervous system struggles to organize all the connection points required for efficient movement.

STRENGTH AS CONNECTION

General strength connects the dots between one segment of the body and the next. When applied thoughtfully, it improves coordination across the entire system by acting like a kind of pliable glue—linking, supporting, and stabilizing as you move.

I taught Megan two dumbbell exercises that immediately improved her shoulder and neck comfort. Dumbbells were simply the right tool for the moment, but we could have easily used the pole, a dish towel, or bodyweight to achieve a similar outcome. The tool matters less than the intention behind it.

Megan needs enough strength to move her body comfortably. She also needs enough to lift and carry objects in daily life, including her 30-pound dog.

WHAT COUNTS AS "HEAVY ENOUGH"?

The key to building general strength is using an input that your body actually recognizes as heavy. That "input" doesn't have to look a certain way or reach a specific number on a weight plate to be effective. It just needs to challenge your current capacity.

MY DEADLIFT DETOUR

Several years ago, I worked with a coach who progressively increased my deadlift load. I had taken a break from lifting heavy to focus on bodyweight movement, but I wanted to regain some of the general strength I'd lost.

At one point, I asked him what the ultimate goal was for my deadlift numbers.

He replied, "Eventually, the goal is to deadlift one and a half times your bodyweight."

Naturally, I had questions. So I did what many of us do—I went to the internet. *Why?* And *says who?*

At the time, I was deadlifting 155 pounds, about 1.22 times my bodyweight, and my body felt great. Nine years later, I still deadlift 155 pounds for reps once a week—and my body still feels great.

According to the internet, including popular media outlets like *Men's Health*, deadlifting 1.5 times your bodyweight is a benchmark for overall strength and fitness.

But realistically, being able to lift 155 pounds four times is probably more than enough for my everyday life. Could I probably pick up 190 pounds (1.5 times my 127-pound bodyweight)? More than likely I could pick it up once. Do I need to? I am not convinced that I do. Most of my clients only need to comfortably lift about half their bodyweight, multiple times, in a variety of shapes and positions, to handle daily activities with ease.

RETHINKING THE NUMBERS

Unless lifting heavy weights is your hobby (or part of your job), training to move large amounts of weight with a barbell is simply a choice. As far as I can tell, it doesn't make a measurable difference in whether someone feels strong, capable, and confident in their ability to perform daily tasks.

The research on how much strength is "enough" is inconsistent at best. Everyone agrees that some strength is necessary, but most studies focus on muscular hypertrophy (building bigger muscles), which isn't everyone's goal.

Interestingly, research suggests a sweet spot around 60 minutes of resistance training per week, with some evidence that more isn't always better—though scientists are still working out exactly why (and when) diminishing returns begin.

THE U-SHAPED CURVE AND THE LIMITS OF RESEARCH

This isn't an area that has been extensively studied, and much of the research behind the U-shaped curve comes from self-reported surveys, which aren't the most reliable source of data.

What *is* clear, however, is that maintaining a certain level of strength adds to your physical armor. If you're a high-level athlete, you'll likely need stronger armor than a 75-year-old who plays golf three times a week and hikes occasionally. But that 75-year-old still needs to be able to carry a golf bag, pick up a ball, and generate enough power and coordination to swing a club effectively.

These skills require a combination of strength, flexibility, and coordination—along with the ability to work smarter, not harder.

LEBRON'S EXAMPLE: BUILDING AN ARMOR THAT LASTS

LeBron James is a basketball legend. He went pro in 2003 at just 18 years old. At the time of this writing, he's preparing for his *23rd* year in the NBA—at 40 years old.

Over his career, he's experienced a few notable injuries (ankle sprain, knee ligament tear, foot tendon tear, and groin strain). But considering he's played for 22 consecutive years, with four championships and 1,562 games (including extended playoff runs), that's remarkable durability.

LeBron lifts weights three days a week. He doesn't do anything overly complicated or spend endless hours in the gym. His strength training serves one primary purpose: to reinforce his *physical armor.*

**James sustained a back injury at the beginning of the 2025 season. He missed the first 14 games, but has been playing consistently since his return.*

A SIMPLE EXPERIMENT

Try this:

- Stand up and imagine there's a box in front of you that's light as a feather.

- Pick it up.

How much tension do you create to lift that imaginary featherweight box?

- Now, imagine the box weighs 110 pounds.

- Pick it up again—still imaginary, of course.

Do you create more or less tension this time?

Most people instinctively create more tension to lift the "heavier" box. Why?

Because your nervous system is smart. When you try to pick up a heavy load, your body automatically creates the necessary *synergistic tension* between the muscles of your torso to resist the pull of the object. Otherwise, that box—real or imagined—would end up back on the floor.

THE MYTH OF THE RIGID SPINE

Despite what many of us have been taught, this doesn't mean the spine needs to remain rigid and unmoving while lifting. In fact, research shows that people's spines often flex naturally when lifting heavy objects—suggesting that spinal movement under load may be a *normal, adaptive phenomenon.*

At this point, you might be wondering: *"But wait—why are we always told to lift with a neutral spine?"*

WHY WE TEACH THE NEUTRAL SPINE

When you're first learning how to build general strength, maintaining a neutral spine is a useful teaching tool. It helps you feel where you're lifting from and develop the *muscular synergy* needed to coordinate your movements safely and effectively.

From a learning perspective, the neutral spine is less about rigidity and more about awareness. It gives you a consistent reference point or an internal feedback system to help you challenge your muscles intentionally through sets and reps.

BALANCING TENSION AND EASE

If you spend a lot of time teaching your body how to create tension, it's equally important to teach it how to move *with less* tension. We need both. But if you lift a featherweight box with the same effort you'd use for a 110-pound one, your body won't feel great over time.

Maybe that's why the weightlifting graph follows a U-shaped curve—and why LeBron James only lifts weights three days a week. Having strength you can easily call upon when needed makes life simpler and your body more resilient. Just as valuable, though, is the ability to move easily—without unnecessary tension or stiffness.

STRENGTH, EFFICIENCY, AND MOVEMENT

Spinal intelligence thrives on strength, but perhaps it benefits even more from efficiency in movement. Efficiency lets you do more of the activities you enjoy. The more you move, the better you tend to feel—both physically and mentally.

Movement creates more movement. And movement that isn't formulaic or exercise-driven, movement done simply for the joy of it, can have a profound impact on your mood, sense of aliveness, and longevity.

DEFINING STRENGTH

It's worth pausing to define what we actually mean by *strength*, since the term gets tossed around constantly by fitness influencers, mind-body teachers, and popular media.

According to my favorite resource, *Merriam-Webster*, **strength** is "the power to resist force." It's the *quality of being strong*—and *strong* means "having great physical power."

By that relatively loose definition, it's no wonder there's no universal agreement on how much strength a person needs. I haven't found a single research paper that definitively states how much weight someone should lift to live a long, fulfilling life.

WHAT THE RESEARCH DOES SAY

There *is* plenty of research showing that strength training positively affects how you feel—both emotionally and physically.

It's been linked to decreases in anxiety and depression, as well as improvements in overall physical function.

If you're reading this and vigorously shaking your head because lifting a barbell changed your life, don't worry—I'm not suggesting there's anything wrong with lifting heavy, especially if you love it. Please, keep going. I still pick up a loaded barbell once or twice a week because it's *fun*.

What I *am* saying is that you don't have to lift large amounts of weight to feel better, move better, or improve your overall health.

And deadlifting 1.5 times your bodyweight? While it might be a cool thing to brag about, it's not a magic elixir for youth, better sex, or an indestructible body.

MANY KINDS OF STRENGTH

Consider these scenarios:

- Is the contact improvisation dancer who lifts people in the air but never lifts weights strong?

- Is the person in Belize who works on a farm, maintains a large hotel property, and guides steep hikes strong?

- Is the mover who carries furniture all day strong?

- Is the parkour athlete who climbs buildings, crawls along railings, and vaults over walls strong?

Of course they are. Strength, like nearly everything else, is *context-dependent*.

If we return to Megan, the pole dancer from the beginning of this chapter, she can do things with her body that a dedicated weightlifter couldn't dream of doing (and might be sore for days if they tried). But her specific strength didn't translate well to the general strength she needed for everyday activities.

Instead of telling her to give up the thing she loves, I gave her a *minimal effective dose* of resistance training to supplement her practice.

If 20–30 minutes of resistance training, two to three times per week, reduces her neck and back pain, and lets her keep dancing, then that's strength doing exactly what it's meant to do.

For many people who don't use their bodies physically every day, a general strength program does more than build muscle. It improves body awareness and, depending on how it's approached, can become a form of mindful exercise. We'll dive deeper into this idea in a moment, but first—how do you know if you might benefit from more general strength?

SELF-CHECK: DO YOU NEED MORE GENERAL STRENGTH?

Use this quick self-assessment to see if a general strength practice might benefit your body and your everyday movement.

STEP 1: REFLECT

Answer each question honestly.

1. Do you regularly lift things that feel moderately heavy—at work, at home, or in the gym?

2. Do you often experience muscle tightness even though you stretch regularly?

3. Do you feel confident picking up or moving the following:

(Give yourself one checkmark for each item you can lift comfortably.)

- ☐ Children or grandchildren
- ☐ Pets
- ☐ A case of water or potting soil
- ☐ A heavy shopping bag
- ☐ Small kitchen appliances (blender, coffee maker, microwave)
- ☐ A potted plant
- ☐ Carry-on luggage

4. Is it difficult to get up and down from the floor?

5. Do you experience low-level neck or low-back pain?

STEP 2: SCORE YOURSELF

- + Give yourself **1 point** for each "yes" to questions 2 through 5.
- − If you answered "yes" to question 1, **subtract 3 points**.

Your total score: ________

Score	What It Means
0 - 1 points	You likely have enough general strength to manage everyday demands. Maintain your current activity level and keep exploring new ways to move.
2 points or higher	You would likely benefit from a general strength program—nothing extreme, just consistent movement that builds resilience, coordination, and confidence in daily life.

A NOTE ON APPROACH

There's no single "right" way to build strength. The best method is the one you enjoy and can sustain.

CrossFit, kettlebells, bodyweight training, resistance machines, Functional Patterns, MovNat, calisthenics—all can be effective when done progressively and safely.

I often use simple exercises with dumbbells, bodyweight, or kettlebells because they're accessible and adaptable, but that doesn't make them superior. Find what fits your environment, personality, and goals—and commit to it.

Earlier, I said I would return to the idea of body awareness and mindfulness. Now feels like a good time to explore this interesting intersection.

The simple act of picking up something heavy improves your body awareness. You can't help but feel your body when you're managing an external load. Your brain registers the pressure of the object in your hands and the resulting strain in your muscles and tendons.

As a result, your **proprioception**, aka your unconscious awareness of where you are in space, kicks into high gear. (The same thing happens when you trail run or flip into a handstand, but I digress.) This heightened awareness strengthens the mind-body connection, especially when you focus on what you're doing.

The focus part is where it gets tricky.

Many people lift or carry moderately heavy things all day without thinking about how they're doing it or what it feels like. A parent picking up a child, friends moving a couch, someone gardening and lifting a pot, or even a person lifting weights at the gym often focus on the task versus the experience of the task.

For most, the act of simply doing works fine. People manage these daily activities without any issues.

But for those who experience discomfort, say, in the wrists, back, or hips, **paying attention** can make a big difference.

Focus connects your mind to your actions. It helps regulate your nervous system and allows you to be present in the moment, *right here, right now.*

I mentioned just a moment ago you can focus on what you are doing, but you can also focus on what you are feeling. They're different. Sometimes, focusing too much on how you feel while moving can disrupt efficient movement—it's like turning attention inward so much that you lose connection to the task itself.

But sometimes focusing on how something feels can give you insight about how you can experience the movement differently. While this wouldn't be the best strategy while trying to lift something really heavy, this can be a useful teaching moment when you are moving at a submaximal effort.

If you think back to Chapter 2, when you identified your shields, one of those shields was meditation. Paying attention to what you're doing isn't exactly the same as quiet stillness, but it *is* a form of mindfulness. You can think of it as **microdosing meditation.** Each moment of attention adds up. Over time, the effects are powerful enough to create another kind of shield.

Paying attention also helps you recognize when something isn't working.

When I talk about the mind-body connection, I mean a **two-way conversation** between the mind and body. Your body communicates clearly if you're willing to listen. It lets you know when to proceed with care and when to push forward. I am always fascinated how people (myself included) just *know* when they can use a heavier weight or they can do another rep.

And sometimes the conscious part of your mind talks you out of something you can actually do. This is when a good coach can be really helpful—they can *see* your potential, even when the voice inside your head is vehemently insisting otherwise.

APPLYING ATTENTION
TO STRENGTH TRAINING

So how can you apply this concept of mindful attention to strength training? Let's return to my client, Megan.

I asked Megan to focus on the position of her spine as she moved the weight. Megan is excellent at moving her spine when she moves her arms. It's an effective strategy—it makes her movement fluid and expressive. But it's also important to be able to move the arms *without* moving the spine, which is what I asked Megan to focus on as she moved her weights.

Having options is key. When you have multiple movement strategies available, your brain will naturally choose the most efficient one for the task at hand. **Having options is part of spinal intelligence.** It creates confidence. And confidence creates trust.

INTEGRATING AWARENESS

The next focal point I gave Megan was to **reach from the back of the armpit to the pinkie finger**. This will make more sense in just a second. Focusing on the pinkie finger reach creates awareness of where the arms are in space and encourages integration of the shoulder blade during the movement.

THE PINKIE REACH

Awareness grows through the edges of sensation. So when you play with sensation through movement, you have an opportunity to grow your awareness.

This practice connects your spine, shoulders, and hands through simple, focused movement. It's designed to integrate the concepts of **attention**, **efficiency**, and **choice**—all key elements of spinal intelligence.

STEP 1: SET UP

Come to a standing position with your feet comfortably apart.

- Soften your knees slightly.

- Let your arms rest by your sides.

- Take a moment to notice your breath and where your weight sits on your feet.

STEP 2: EXPLORE THE THUMB REACH

1. Reach one arm overhead, leading with your **thumb**.

2. Pause briefly at the top.

3. Lower your arm slowly.

4. Repeat two or three times.

Notice: How does this feel through your shoulder, neck, and torso? Does your spine move?

STEP 3: EXPLORE THE PINKIE REACH

1. Now reach the same arm overhead, but this time lead with your **pinkie finger**.

2. Pause at the top again.

3. Lower your arm slowly and repeat two or three times.

Notice: Which version feels smoother or more "spacious"?

Does one direction create a sense of ease or openness in your movement?

Most people find that leading with the pinkie finger feels easier, with more room in the joint for movement. This subtle shift changes how the shoulder blade and spine work together—less effort, more integration.

STEP 4: INTEGRATE AWARENESS

As you move, bring your attention to:

- The relationship between your **arm and spine**.

- The connection from the **back of your armpit** to your **pinkie finger**.

- The way your body naturally coordinates the motion when you focus.

This is the same principle Megan used in her strength training: **using attention to organize the movement from within**.

What did you notice?

- Where did you feel the movement begin?

- Did you sense any difference in effort, balance, or stability?

- How might this awareness translate to lifting, carrying, or daily movement?

Use the space below to record your observations.

____

____

____

____

TIP

You can apply this same focus to nearly any strength or mobility exercise. Next time you lift something—whether it's a dumbbell, a grocery bag, or your child—pause for a moment to *feel* where the movement begins, how your spine responds, and whether you have multiple options for the task.

That awareness is spinal intelligence in action.

TRAINING THE BRAIN
THROUGH MOVEMENT

By asking Megan to focus on the position of her spine and the direction of her reach, several regions of her brain worked together. Her mind was less likely to wander, and her nervous system received rich sensory feedback.

Reaching from the pinkie side of the hand to the outer edge of the armpit created a specific sensation she can use in other contexts.

By the end of the exercise, she had stressed her muscles in a new way by strengthening the tissues around her neck and learned something new about how to move her arm. The exercise was beneficial for both her **body and her brain.**

REFLECTION: YOUR RELATIONSHIP WITH STRENGTH

Take a few minutes to explore your personal connection to strength training. There are no right or wrong answers—just curiosity.

Step 1: Reflect

When was the last time you devoted 20 minutes, twice a week, to resistance training?

____

If you already train regularly, what motivates you to do it?

- ☐ Habit or routine
- ☐ Physical appearance
- ☐ Mental health or stress relief
- ☐ Curiosity / experimentation
- ☐ Strength for sport or art
- ☐ Daily function and longevity
- ☐ Other: _________________________________

How do you feel before and after strength training?

____

Step 2: Connect

Think back to what you learned earlier about *attention* and *spinal intelligence*.

• Where does your focus usually go when you lift—your breath, your effort, or something else?

• What happens to your spine and your sense of "space" when you move with attention versus autopilot?

BARRIERS TO STRENGTH TRAINING

If you don't currently resistance train, what might be getting in the way?

Look over the list below and place a check mark next to each statement that applies to you.

- ☐ I'm not sure what exercises to do

- ☐ I've never lifted weights before and don't know how to start

- ☐ I find the weight room intimidating

- ☐ I don't know how much weight to lift

- ☐ I don't know how many sets or reps to do

- ☐ I don't have time

- ☐ I would rather be doing something else

- ☐ I don't like being sore

If any of these feel familiar—and you scored two or higher on the self-check earlier in this chapter—then you'd likely benefit from a simple, adaptable strength training program, like the one at the end of the Chapter.

WHY LIGHTER IS SMARTER (AT FIRST)

You'll probably need to purchase heavier dumbbells sooner rather than later. One of the first things that happens when you begin any kind of exercise program is that your motor cortex, the part of the brain responsible for planning and coordinating voluntary movement, recognizes that you're doing something that requires more effort than usual.

Your brain then rallies the troops by:

- Recruiting more motor units within your muscles.

- Coordinating those motor units to fire more synchronously.

- Improving communication between limbs and joints.

This means you get stronger quickly—not because your muscles suddenly grow, but because your **coordination improves**. And coordination is a brain thing, not a body thing.

This is one reason why starting with light weights to learn the movements, then gradually increasing the load, can be so beneficial.

THE CASE OF BETH

I have a client I'll call *Beth*. She's extremely flexible and had chronic neck pain, precipitated by a car accident 30 years ago.

When we began, every time I added weight, something flared up. I realized I was progressing too quickly, so I scaled back. Way back. Instead of five-pound dumbbells, we used twos. Instead of an eight-pound medicine ball, we used an unweighted ball.

From there, Beth progressed steadily: five pounds, eight, then ten, eventually lifting twenty-six pounds with ease (and for context, she weighs 102 pounds). She also began leg pressing more than forty pounds and using machines that had previously caused discomfort—some of which we initially did *without any weight at all*.

When we reflected on her journey recently, Beth said I was "really good at modifying." I think what she meant was that I met her where she was.

Anyone can build strength if they're willing to start at a level that challenges them *without overwhelming their system.*

Strength, like so many other things in life, is relative.

GUARDRAILS, SHIELDS, AND PERCEPTION

People who've experienced many **insults**—physical injuries, chronic stress, emotional strain—may need to start with less weight than those with more **shields** (protective habits, support systems, and resilience).

The nervous system sets up guardrails, both mental and physical, when faced with something new.

- Someone with a lot of shields tends to see new experiences as safe or manageable.

- Someone with a lot of insults tends to see new experiences as potentially threatening.

When movement feels threatening, the body overreacts by bracing, tensing, and working harder than necessary.

Bracing isn't always bad, and sometimes bracing serves a purpose—if you were about to accidentally step off a cliff, every ounce of your being would brace to hold you back.

The trouble with chronic bracing is it limits fluidity. It's like trying to drive with the parking brake on.

When I gave Beth a load so light it was barely perceptible, she stopped bracing. Her body figured out the appropriate amount of tension for the task.

Once she became more coordinated and comfortable, the same weight felt too easy. She was ready to progress—because her relationship to the task had changed.

STRENGTH AS PART OF A MOVEMENT DIET

Think of the movement component of **spinal intelligence** as a well-balanced diet. Resistance training is your **protein**.

Just like 10–35% of your daily calories should come from protein, about **10–35% of your weekly movement time** should come from resistance training.

To put this a different way, if you move about five hours a week (roughly 300 minutes), resistance training should make up **30 to 105 minutes** of that time.

Since movement happens everywhere, not just in the gym, you don't necessarily need to just lift weights in the gym to meet your weekly resistance training allotment.

If you regularly lift firewood, haul garden soil, or carry lumber, you may already be meeting your "protein" requirement. But if you work at a desk and spend your downtime reading or sitting, you'll benefit from more dedicated strength work.

FINDING THE RIGHT DOSE

Before anyone gets huffy and insists 30 minutes isn't enough for a "real" strength program, let me remind you **the best exercise is the one you'll actually do.**

Two 15-minute sessions a week are infinitely better than none.

And for many people, shorter, more focused sessions are both *physically* and *mentally* more sustainable than hour-long gym routines.

As we discussed earlier with the U-shaped curve, your goal is to find the **optimal dose**—enough to support your body and life without tipping into fatigue or overuse.

Too little resistance training and you feel kind of like Bambi, gangly, slightly uncoordinated, and hopeful someone else will do the heavy lifting. Too much resistance training and you feel more like the Hulk—invincible as long as you aren't asked to move fast or pick something up off the floor. Just like eating only protein can make you sluggish, an exercise diet that's *only* resistance training can leave you stiff and disconnected.

Your body—and your brain—thrive on balance.

A SIMPLE, ADAPTABLE STRENGTH ROUTINE

Below is a short resistance training program. Each exercise includes two or three **focal points** to help you connect strength with awareness.

Try the focal points that resonate most with you, and notice how they affect the quality of your movement.

PRACTICE: A SAMPLE STRENGTH TRAINING SESSION

This short strength session integrates physical effort with mindful attention.

You can complete it at home with two sets of dumbbells—one light, one moderately heavy.

Before you begin, take a moment to check in.

STEP 1: RATE HOW YOU FEEL

On a scale of 1–5, note how you feel before you start:

Tired		Neutral		Energized & ready to move
1	2	3	4	5

At the end of your session, rate yourself again.

Did anything shift? More energy, more ease, less tension?

STEP 2: WARM-UP

Cat/Cow: 6–8 rounds

- Focus on initiating the movement from different parts of your spine each round.

Shoulder Rolls: 4–6 repetitions

- Begin by keeping your spine still.

- After 2–4 rolls, allow the spine to move with your shoulders.

Standing Spine Rotation with Arm Swing: 4–6 repetitions

- Start by initiating the twist from your **breastbone**.

- After a few rounds, lead the rotation from your **pelvis**.

Total Body Shaking: 30 seconds

- Shake out your arms, legs, and torso to release residual tension.

Single-Arm Bench Row *(moderate weight)*

- Press the supporting hand and knee firmly into the bench.

- Keep the back of your head and throat long.

- Initiate the pull with your **elbow**.

Push-Up *(choose variation: hands elevated, knees down, or full)*

- Maintain an imaginary line between your **breastbone and pubic bone** as you lower and rise.

- Rotate your hands **away** from each other as you lower, and **toward** each other as you push up.

- Focus on **pulling yourself down** rather than just pushing up.

Box Squat *(weight optional)*

- Maintain the connection between your breastbone and pubic bone.

- Sense how your weight shifts across your feet.

- Keep your gaze steady on a spot in front of you.

STEP 4: **SETS 3-4**

Split-Stance Squat *(weight optional)*

- Feel both feet connecting with the ground.

- Reach the back knee toward the floor.

- Shift your weight over the front foot as you lower.

Suitcase Deadlift (from top position) *(moderately heavy weight)*

- Reach the weight toward the **outside of your shins**.

- Hold with your **hands, not fingers**.

- Keep your eyes focused slightly forward.

Single-Arm Chest Press *(moderate weight)*

- Feel your **ribs** resting against the floor.

- Keep your **feet grounded**.

- Let your **elbow touch** the ground gently at the bottom of each rep.

When you finish, pause and notice:

- How does your body feel now compared to when you began?

- What part of your body feels most alive or aware?

- Did a particular focal point help you move more easily?

Write down a few quick notes below.

____

____

____

____

> **TIP**
>
> You can complete this session two or three times per week.
>
> It's simple by design—enough to build coordination, strength, and awareness without taking too much time. Even though it takes some effort to learn the movements, once you know them, it won't be too mentally taxing.
>
> As you progress, adjust the weights, tempo, or repetitions, but keep your **focal points** and **attention** at the center of practice.

CHAPTER 4:
FLEXIBILITY REFRAMED

—

I have a client I'll call **Margot.** Margot is incredibly strong and always on the move. She has boundless energy and can often be found hauling heavy pots around her garden, walking her sixty-pound Labrador retriever, or tackling projects around the house.

A few years ago, while cleaning up after Thanksgiving, Margot ran into an open dishwasher door. The fall was spectacular—she tore several muscles in her right shoulder.

An orthopedic surgeon told her she would likely need a partial shoulder replacement, but she could try physical therapy first to see how it went.

"Physical therapy," she replied without hesitation.

She completed sixteen weeks of physical therapy. During that time, I worked with her on maintaining body awareness (because injuries do weird things to your physical sense of self), improving spinal movement, and transferring weight through her feet. I also had her keep her uninjured arm strong and keep up her leg strength.

After she finished her sessions with the physical therapist, I continued working with her to integrate movement through her spine and arms. Her progress continued steadily, but the real turning point came when I asked if I could create a ten-minute video routine for her to do each morning.

"That would be wonderful," she said.

Margot did that ten-minute routine every day—and the progress was remarkable, even to me. She regained her full range of motion. Since then, I've made three more ten-minute videos for her, and she continues to do one daily, unless she's meeting with me in person.

Margot is seventy-nine years old. Her routine consists primarily of gentle, full-body movement and flexibility work, with a bit of strength thrown in—and it continues to serve her well.

THE CASE FOR FLEXIBILITY

There are a lot of people right now shouting about the importance of strength from the rooftop or, more accurately, TikTok. As you saw in the last chapter, they aren't wrong: strength is incredibly important. But so is being able to move easily.

For people who are always on the go and are already strong, like Margot, emphasizing movement quality, flexibility, and learning to move easily can pack a bigger punch than a traditional strength training program. Those of us with high energy and a constant drive to *do* often use more effort than they need. It's kind of like riding a ten-speed bike in the highest gear all the time—the pedals turn slowly as you grind your way forward, even though several lower gears are available that would make pedaling feel smoother (and easier).

A lot of people think of flexibility as stretching, but flexibility is actually the ability to bend without breaking. While it's true that flexibility can improve with strength training, this effect is most pronounced in people who haven't been exercising regularly. For someone like Margot, who already has a baseline of strength and fitness, lifting weights alone wasn't going to restore the coordination between her shoulder and torso.

Lifting weights also doesn't do much to teach easeful movement. As soon as you pick up a weight, you tell yourself a story about what that weight represents and what you're supposed to *do* (and *feel*) with it. That story influences how much tension you create and how you move. This tension can be useful, but, like the high gear on a bike, you don't need it all the time. In fact, most of the time, you probably don't (but in those moments when you *do* need it, you're glad it's available).

Ideally, when you set the weight down, you stop generating so much tension and return to a more easeful way of moving. Some of us, however, keep the tension on, as though we're still pedaling in high gear even after the terrain has changed—grinding our way uphill when it would be better to shift down and move with less resistance.

When I was in my twenties, my entire body felt like a giant electrical circuit. Based on the low level hum I felt all of the time, I was pretty sure if I could figure out a way to harness my nervous system, I could power an entire apartment building (or at least my unit, which, back then, would have been a welcome reduction in my PG&E bill). Despite the fact that I was doing triathlons, lifting weights, and practicing yoga, my body hurt. It didn't know how to relax and I only had one speed—fast.

Fortunately, I learned some things. I'm forty-six now, and my body feels great. I still lift weights and run, but I also learned how to dance, studied a variety of mind-body disciplines, and figured out how to pick up a pencil without using the same amount of effort as if I were picking up a 155-pound barbell.

People often equate flexibility training with holding stretches for minutes on end. Depending on your goals, that kind of stretching can be helpful, but for many of us, simply learning to move in a more relaxed way is enough to improve flexibility and help the body feel more balanced (especially when it comes to flexibility through the spine).

HOW MUCH FLEXIBILITY DO YOU NEED?

One of the most common shoulder complaints I hear from people is that it hurts when they reach behind them. Why?

You need shoulder flexibility to reach behind you, but you also need your spine to rotate as well. Otherwise, it's like you are trying to cram an extra pair of socks in your sock drawer without taking a pair out. Flexibility requires having space to move into; if your arm has no space behind you to move, things get jammed up (and that doesn't always feel great).

TRY THIS:

Reach behind you as though you're grabbing something from the backseat of your car. Look toward where you're reaching with your eyes and let your chest rotate in that direction.

Now try the same movement without turning your torso or looking where you're reaching.

Which one feels better?

Usually, looking and rotating your torso feels better. When you look, rotate, and reach, you maximize the space you have to move. Your spine, specifically your neck and rib cage, helps you rotate, sharing the path of the movement across multiple areas rather than just moving from your shoulder.

Have you ever tried to lift a heavy object overhead, like a heavy bag you are throwing into the overhead luggage compartment on the airplane, and had your back feel like it tweaked?

You aren't alone. This is one of those complaints I hear semi-regularly. When you press something heavy overhead, again, something has to get out of the way. If you don't think about how you do this, often the thing that gets out of the way if your low back. (And this doesn't always feel very good.)

TRY THIS:

Pretend you're holding a heavy object with both hands. Push the imaginary object overhead, letting your low back arch as you do it.

Now, try again, but this time, keep your low back in place as you push the imaginary object overhead.

Which feels better?

Usually, pushing without arching your back feels more stable. Why?

When you keep your lumbar spine anchored, your torso muscles support that stability, allowing your arms to do the pushing. This creates a stronger platform to initiate the lift. If the object is really heavy, your torso might still contribute by arching or bending at the very end, helping you get that last bit of oomph to lift it fully overhead.

Instead of being the catalyst for the movement, your back becomes the assistant to the movement.

When you learn how to *feel* when your spine is moving, it becomes easier to notice when it isn't (and vice versa). This awareness improves your coordination and gives your brain a clearer picture of what's happening and when.

Some movements work better when the spine moves freely; others work better when the spine stays more stable. But regardless of whether the spine is moving or not moving, it's an integral part of every movement you make.

If you want to move in a way that feels easeful and integrated, but aren't sure how, ask yourself the following questions:

- Do I have a clear image of what I'm trying to do?

- Does the movement feel safe?

- Do I know how to coordinate the movement?

- Do I have good sensory input?

For many people, addressing these four areas makes a huge difference in their flexibility. If you want to be a contortionist, you'll need some extra components—but if your goal isn't to touch your head to your heels, running through this checklist whenever you do a flexibility or mobility exercise is an excellent place to start.

A CLEAR IMAGE
AND A SENSE OF SAFETY

We fear what we don't understand. It's a normal human response—and it applies to movement, too.

If you're working on your flexibility but aren't clear on *what* you're trying to do in a specific position or movement, how well do you think it goes?

Not very. There's usually some awkwardness as you figure out where to put your limbs, coupled with the tension that naturally arises when you're unsure of what you're doing (performance anxiety is a very real thing, even if you are learning a movement in your living room by yourself). I always find it interesting how many people expect to be able to do a new movement or exercise perfectly the first time, even if they have never done it before.

DOES THE MOVEMENT FEEL SAFE?

Simone Biles is considered one of the greatest female gymnasts of all time. When she was first learning a Tkatchev, a move on the uneven bars where you release and regrasp the same bar, she hit the bar on one of her attempts. The experience scared her, proving that even people who seem superhuman have limits around what risks they are willing to take. As a result, she didn't attempt that move again for quite some time.

Instead, she went back to the fundamentals. She practiced the foundational drills that helped her regain comfort and orientation on the bars. By returning to the basics, she gave herself the chance to relearn where she was trying to go, so that when she tried the skill again (with a spotter), she knew what to expect, not just visually, but *in her body*.

This ties directly into whether a movement feels safe. If you don't know where you're going or what to expect, the movement feels uncertain and, in some instances, scary. If you have a negative experience with something the very first time you try it, your emotional response can hinder the learning process, at least for some people.

Other people view the negative experience as a challenge. The negative first experience becomes a starting point to grow from, rather than an insurmountable obstacle.

When I was first learning aerial silks, I attended a class that consisted of two adults and twelve children between the ages of 8 and 12. The teacher got excited because I am strong and taught me a circle drop.

The drop consists of climbing up high enough that you don't hit your head when you drop. You wrap your legs in a specific way so you are secure and then you hurl your head towards the ground, throwing your body in a circle.

It was petrifying, to put it mildly. I was pretty sure I was going to die, and when I didn't die, I was pretty sure I never wanted to do that again.

Three months later, my regular teacher told me it was time for me to learn the circle drop. Initially, I balked. I had zero interest in doing that again.

After practicing the wrap a few times and with a little coaxing (or maybe a lot of coaxing), I decided maybe trying it again wouldn't be that bad. It was still scary, but not as scary as the first time.

I kept practicing and learning, and eventually the circle drop became a non-issue, something I could just do without feeling one way or another about it. But that initial experience stayed with me a long time.

You may have come up with different words for each situation. In the second scenario, many people (myself included) feel nervous about slipping or falling.

How does that change how you move?

When I'm unsure about my footing, I tend to brace and stiffen because I don't know what the ground will feel like when my foot lands—which, ironically, makes my balance worse.

So what do I do?

I shorten my stride.

I focus on breathing.

I lean slightly forward so I'm moving *with* the incline instead of against it.

I return to the basics.

Scenarios like this can become *insults* if you fall and injure yourself, or *shields* if you learn to work with the situation instead of against it.

Simone Biles has repeatedly confronted fear and performed seemingly impossible skills. She does it by breaking the complex into smaller, manageable parts. These are the pieces she feels comfortable practicing alone, and then she uses a spotter for safety and feedback.

With consistent practice and time, she becomes comfortable practicing more pieces alone and becomes less reliant on the spotter until eventually, she is able to perform the move on her own. It might still induce a little bit of fear, but she can execute it without bracing.

You might be wondering what this has to do with flexibility.

If there's fear around a specific movement, maybe because you don't have a clear image of what you're trying to do, or the position doesn't feel safe, it's usually for one of three reasons:

1. You don't know what to expect.

2. You've had a bad experience with that movement or position before.

3. You don't yet know *how* to do it.

The solution isn't to force your body to touch your toes or push your arms overhead. The solution is to find the elements of the movement you *can* do—and build from there.

DO YOU KNOW HOW TO COORDINATE THE MOVEMENT, AND DO YOU HAVE GOOD SENSORY INPUT?

You don't know what you don't know.

If someone asks you to sit down with your legs extended forward and touch your toes, but you haven't done that since your P.E. middle school teacher was all excited about the sit and reach, it probably won't feel great. Unless you're naturally bendy, that position might even feel impossible.

And if someone asked you to explain how you got into that position, would you be able to articulate the steps?

Unless you've spent time really thinking about *how* you move, probably not. Very few of us pay attention to the process behind our everyday movements—we just do them.

This isn't a bad thing, but it does make it tricky when you want to sense, feel, and explore movement in a different way.

> **REFLECTION**
>
> *Before moving on, take a moment to write down three different ways you could come into a seated forward bend.*
>
> *(I'll offer three examples at the end of the chapter.)*
>
> 1. ____
>
> 2. ____
>
> 3. ____

Learning how to coordinate movement requires being able to **sense and feel where different parts of your body are in space**, and then being able to use those parts in an organized way.

Over the next few pages, we'll explore several common techniques people use to improve flexibility and discuss *why* they work.

TAPPING:
COLORING IN THE MAP OF YOU

"I saw this tapping technique on social media. I tried it, and it solved all of my problems."

While no one has actually said this to me, I've seen versions of that statement floating around online.

Tapping is a technique that has been used by Qi Gong practitioners for hundreds of years. It's simple: you tap or lightly slap different parts of your body with your hands, moving up and down the skin as you go.

This has several positive effects. The act of tapping or slapping applies **pressure,** which gives the brain clear sensory input about where that part of the body is located. You can think of it as coloring in the map of *you* that exists in your brain.

The clearer and more colorful the map, the easier it is to navigate—to know where you are and where you want to go.

Tapping or rubbing the skin also creates **vibration** that travels through the body. Cells communicate through vibration; in fact, when cells stop vibrating, they stop functioning properly. (More on this in Chapter 5.) Enhancing cellular vibration throughout your body may help support vitality and responsiveness.

The right amount of pressure creates just enough vibration to stimulate your nervous system without overwhelming it. An appropriately stimulated nervous system for what you are doing or what you are about to do is a *balanced* nervous system.

And when there's balance, there's an element of ease. Ease creates freedom of movement.

Tapping or slapping also provides an **external focus** for your attention. This temporarily quiets the internal dialogue many of us have running throughout the day, restoring internal balance. Balanced mind, balanced body.

The result? You'll likely feel more flexible—at least temporarily. Tapping opens a window of opportunity: a moment to move more, and with less tension.

OTHER INTERIM SHIELDS

Tapping is just one example of what I call an *interim shield*—a simple, temporary tool that helps create safety, balance, and awareness. Here are a few others:

- **Foam rolling.** A form of self-myofascial massage that involves applying pressure to different parts of the body. This can be done with a foam roller, a small rubber ball, or, if you like more intensity, a lacrosse ball. Like tapping, it's a form of pressure therapy. It temporarily reduces discomfort and brings attention to specific areas of your body.

- **Breathing.** Breathwork focuses attention, enhances awareness, and influences internal pressure—all of which affect how you move. Depending on how it's taught, breathing can bring your focus to different regions of the body and help calm or energize the nervous system.

- **Eye drills.** Eye movements can be practiced in many ways and typically involve focusing on an external object. Vision work can be especially beneficial for people who tend to focus internally. The brain area that processes visual information is different from the one that organizes movement, but the two are connected by something called the **dorsal stream**.

Performing vision drills helps prime that pathway, allowing the visual and movement systems to share the input. This creates a kind of balance between interpreting internal sensations and responding to the external environment.

Each of these practices helps **build awareness, coordination, and safety—** key ingredients for improving flexibility in a meaningful way.

EXPLORING INTERIM SHIELDS

Look at the chart below.

Place a mark next to what each *interim shield* does.

Then, place a mark next to what *you* could use more of in your own movement practice.

All of these interim shields reduce sensations of tension.

They are also beneficial for creating a short-term improvement in flexibility, for many of the same reasons mentioned earlier.

REFLECTION ACTIVITY

Interim Shield	Focused Attention	Pressure	Flexibility	External Awareness
Tapping	☐	☐	☐	☐
Foam Rolling	☐	☐	☐	☐
Eye Drills	☐	☐	☐	☐
Breathing	☐	☐	☐	☐

Now glance back at the list. Which of these would be easiest for you to incorporate as a supplement to your movement or exercise practice?

A QUICK NOTE ON BREATHING

All of these interim shields affect your nervous system, which means they also temporarily influence your range of motion.

Breathing, in particular, can have a powerful effect. Certain types of breathing can shift your nervous system from a balanced sympathetic/parasympathetic state to a predominantly parasympathetic one. Or to a predominantly sympathetic one. The breathing exercise you choose depends on what you are trying to do.

When you use breathing to influence your parasympathetic state, instead of feeling awake, alert, and calmly focused, you may feel ready to take a nap—which isn't ideal if you're about to start a workout or give an important presentation (unless either of them involves napping).

I teach parasympathetic breathing techniques frequently in workshops, but I usually save those exercises for the *end* of the workshop, not the beginning. That way, people leave feeling relaxed, like they have had a natural martini, which is a good note to leave on.

All of this is to say: how you sequence and implement different techniques, drills, and exercises matters.

TIMING AND FOCUS

During a recent handstand course I taught, I incorporated eye drills halfway through one of the sessions.

Handstands are both literally and figuratively a narrowly focused skill, and the eye drills served as a reset, shifting participants' attention and energy. When they returned to their handstand practice, they were more balanced, both mentally and physically. Instead of relying just on proprioception, they were temporarily able to rely more on their visual input.

These interim shields that I just mentioned—tapping, breathing, eye drills, can be thought of as *nervous system hacks.*

But like all hacks, unless you back them up with something more substantial, the results are temporary.

All sensory inputs influence movement output. While they can impact how you coordinate movement, sometimes simply focusing on *what you're doing* and how it feels can also have a profound effect.

ANOTHER WAY TO THINK OF THIS:

All of these sensory inputs influence how you express movement.

And just like with emotions, the greater your range of expression, the less limited you feel.

COORDINATION AND PRECISION

Coordination is the ability to produce precise movements through the planning and execution of specific joint actions. Different activities require different levels of coordination.

Does it take more coordination to walk on a predictable, flat surface or to hit a baseball?

Most of us can agree that it probably takes more coordination to hit a baseball. You need to coordinate your swing at exactly the right time with a specific sequence of movements to connect the bat with the ball.

When you're first learning a movement, the focus is on *global coordination*—figuring out how to organize yourself enough to perform the desired action.

This is where you:

- Figure out where you're going.

- Practice in the safest way possible.

- Learn how to generate the right balance between ease and tension.

Once you can comfortably perform the general movement pattern, you can shift toward *specific coordination*.

Coordination, remember, is about creating a desired action—it's not passive. It requires doing.

If you can't feel a specific aspect of the movement, slow down. Pause. Notice what it's like to be in that position.

But ultimately, the act of actually moving is what develops true coordination.

FLEXIBILITY **IN MOTION**

Flexibility is often viewed as the ability to make shapes.

Making shapes can be fun—and it can have value—but when you're moving, making a shape isn't what determines whether your movement is effective. Coordination does.

Coordination is the ultimate expression of movement.

Simone Biles performing a beam routine and Babe Ruth swinging a baseball bat are both incredible examples of coordination. Each requires strength, flexibility, and balance, but more importantly, both demand the ability to fully express range under pressure.

Flexibility is so much more than making shapes. It can act as another *shield* when it's applied in a way that balances stress and relaxation during specific tasks.

Some people find holding static positions and shapes relaxing. Usually these individuals have a fair amount of natural flexibility. They can flop forward in a pancake stretch and hang out there comfortably, relaxing into the stretch. The rest of us experience better results when we approach flexibility through *movement*—moving in and out of positions in ways that cultivate openness and curiosity.

Flexibility isn't all you need, but it's a natural byproduct of exploring movement—especially when that movement includes rotating, reaching, and folding. Contrary to the stereotype that athletes of earlier eras didn't train, Babe Ruth worked extensively with New York fitness trainer Artie McGovern starting in 1925 and published his own series of fitness articles documenting roughly sixty exercises, including calisthenics and bat-based movement work. Simone Biles included stretching in her warm-ups, but it was performing the movements themselves—releasing from the bars, coming into a standing split on a beam—that developed the coordination required to perform at the highest level.

PRACTICE LIBRARY

Below are **five short flexibility** practices that incorporate the concepts discussed throughout this chapter.

There are many ways to approach each exercise; the descriptions below are simply one option.

As you move, ask yourself:

- Do I understand what I'm trying to do?

- Are there any parts of the exercises where I feel uncertain about where I'm going?

- How could I approach this exercise differently?

(I'll offer examples of different approaches in the next chapter. You can also find the practices with photos in Chapter 8.)

PRACTICE 1: FOCUS ON THE SHOULDERS

1. **Rub and Sense.** Begin standing. Rub the skin around your chest, shoulders, and down your arms.

2. **Shift and Draw.** Stand with your feet wide. As you shift your weight side to side, draw a large, horizontal figure 8 with your right arm. Let your hand trace it. Then your elbow. Then your shoulder. Repeat with the left arm.

3. **Slide.** With feet comfortably apart, slide your shoulders up and down. Then, see if you can move only the *shoulder blades* up and down.

4. **Eyes and Arms.** Make a thumbs-up with your right hand. Lift it to eye level. Keep your head still as you move your right arm out to the side, keeping your eyes fixed on the thumb. When you lose sight of it, bring the hand back to the start. Repeat 2–4 times. Then, repeat while allowing your head to follow. Repeat both versions with your left hand.

5. **Wrap and Reach.** Slide your hands to your elbows. Reach the elbows forward, rounding your spine and head. Then, lift the elbows up and overhead, as though taking off a sweater.

1. **Spinal Mapping.** Begin on hands and knees. Move your breastbone up toward the ceiling, then toward the floor. Move your belly toward the ceiling, then toward the floor. Finally, bring your shoulders and hips as close together as possible in the front, then in the back.

2. **Rock and Reach.** Feel your hands against the ground. Rock your hips toward your heels and back several times. As you rock back, reach your right hand a little farther forward, then the left. Do 2–3 rounds.

3. **Rest and Breathe.** Sit hips back toward your heels. Take 2–4 breaths, imagining the breath filling the space between your shoulder blades.

4. **Rotation Flow.** Return to hands and knees. Float your knees slightly off the floor. Turn your knees to the right as you pick up your right hand and place it behind you—the eyes now face the horizon. Turn back to the left, returning the right hand to the floor. Repeat to the other side. Pause with hands behind you, eyes on the horizon. Let your chest sink, then expand. Do 2–3 times.

5. **Side Prop.** Lie on your right side with knees bent, propped on your right hand. Let your right ribs drop toward the floor, then lift away a few times. Keeping the ribs lifted, reach your left hand toward the ceiling. Begin small arm circles. Repeat on the other side.

PRACTICE 3: **SPINE**

1. **Bounce and Feel.** Begin standing. Lightly bounce up and down for 30 seconds, noticing the vibration through your body.

2. **Dive and Roll.** Imagine an invisible wall in front of you. Dive under it, then extend up the other side. Do 3–4 times. Reverse the direction—extend down and roll back up.

3. **Circle the Space.** Stand with feet wide, as if holding a large beach ball. Move the "ball" in a big circle, touching the floor, walls, and ceiling. Perform 4–5 circles in one direction, then switch. Does one direction feel easier?

4. **Wall Rotation.** Place your hands on a wall with fingers pointing away from each other. Step your right foot behind your left as you rotate your

body away from the wall (the right hand lifts). Return to start, rotating back toward the wall—foot, hips, chest. Which sequence feels most natural? Repeat on the other side.

5. **Breathing Around the Ball.** Imagine your arms wrapped around a large beach ball. As you inhale, open the arms away from the ball. As you exhale, return the arms to wrap around it. Repeat 3–5 times.

PRACTICE 4: **SINE AND HIPS**

1. **Round and Extend.** On hands and knees, round your back as you reach hips back. Extend your back as you shift hips forward. Repeat 2–4 times.

2. **Slide and Feel.** Take knees slightly wider. Slide your feet to the right as you sit hips back. Return to center as you bring hips forward. Notice what your back does as you move. After 4–6 rounds, slide and reach hips back until you come into a seated 90/90 position. Repeat to the other side.

3. **Roll and Rise.** From 90/90 with right knee in front, extend your left leg. Place your right hand on the floor slightly behind the right hip (fingers can point away from you). Turn your palm up toward the ceiling and bring your cheek toward your palm, rolling onto your side. Continue rolling onto your back. Return by bringing your cheek to your palm and pressing yourself back up. Do 2–4 times, then switch sides.

What does your spine have to do to lower you? What helps you come back up? How can your extended leg make it easier?

PRACTICE 5: **HIPS AND FEET**

1. **Knee Circles.** Stand with hands on knees. Circle the knees 3–4 times each direction.

2. **Walk the Hands.** Slide hands down your shins to the floor, walking them forward a few steps. Let your knees reach toward the floor (they might even touch). Walk your hands back to lift the knees and return upright. Repeat 2–4 times.

3. **Shift and Lift.** From hands and knees, walk your hands around your knees to the right, shifting weight back until the knees lift off the ground. Lower and repeat 2–4 times.

4. **Slide and Reach.** From hands and knees, keep the skin of your left foot on the floor as you slide it straight back. Once extended, reach it out to the left—keeping contact with the floor. Do 2–4 times. On the final repetition, slide the foot out and shift hips back as you lift your chest and hands. Slide hands back down to the floor and return to start. Repeat 2–4 times.

5. **Seated Weight Shift.** Sit with your right foot on the floor (knee pointing up) and your left foot tucked behind the right knee. Sit on support if needed. Reach your right knee forward, using your hands on the floor to help you weight-shift. Feel the weight travel into the ball of your right foot. Return to start. Repeat 2–4 times, then switch sides. *Option:* After reaching the knee forward several times, reach it forward and to the left so it aligns with the left knee. Sit back on your heels or remain upright. Reverse the movement to return.

THREE WAYS TO COME INTO A SEATED FORWARD FOLD

Option 1:

- Sit on a pillow or folded blanket with legs extended and knees slightly bent.

- Hold the backs of your knees.

- Roll your sitting bones back as you reach your torso forward over your legs.

- Roll your sitting bones under as you return upright.

- Repeat 3–5 times. On the last one, hold for 3 breaths.

Option 2:

- Wear socks on a smooth surface. Sit with knees bent, holding the backs of your thighs.

- Keep your chest reaching toward your knees as you slide your heels away from you.

- If you lose that chest-to-knee connection, slide the heels back in.

- Repeat 3–5 times. Hold the last position for 3 breaths.

Option 3:

- Lie on your back. Lift your hips toward the ceiling, rolling onto your mid-back.

- Roll up into a seated position with legs extended, reaching your hands toward your feet.

- Roll back down, hips toward the ceiling.

- Repeat 3–5 times, exhaling as you roll.

Take a moment to reflect on the three seated forward fold options you just practiced.

Notice which version felt easiest, which felt most effective, and which gave you the clearest sense of what you were doing.

There are no right or wrong answers—just information about how you move, how you sense, and how you respond.

1. Which option did you prefer?

2. Why?

3. Which one felt most successful?

As you reflect, consider how your comfort, coordination, and sense of safety influenced your choice.

These are the same elements that shape flexibility in all forms of movement.

CHAPTER 5:
COORDINATION OVER CORRECTION

—

"I wanted to ask you—what do you think about my back structure issue?"

"What issue is that?"

"My anterior pelvic tilt. I've been told it's a problem."

There's a strong desire, as human beings, to fix things and make them better. In the world of fitness, rehabilitation, and movement, we're always looking for ways to help people feel better in their bodies. But sometimes, that search leads us down rabbit holes of imaginary or exaggerated issues. What the back *should* or *shouldn't* look like is one of those rabbit holes that, unfortunately, became a mainstream myth.

I talked about the natural curves of the spine in Chapter 1, but to quickly recap: between your head and shoulders, your spine curves forward. Between your shoulders and ribs, it curves backward. Between your ribs and pelvis, it curves forward again—creating an "S" shape when viewed from the side.

The word *anterior* means "toward the front of the body." Your pelvis is connected to the bottom of your spine, and it moves forward and backward based on how your spine moves. (It can also move side to side, and around in a circle. If you are unsure about all of the ways your pelvis can move, pull up a video of a salsa dancer. Like Shakira wisely noted, hips don't lie.)

Since the lower spine naturally curves forward, the pelvis naturally tips forward in many positions, especially when you're moving forward. So an anterior pelvic tilt isn't an issue. It's *simply* a position. In fact, it's a position you move in and out of regularly throughout the day. If you don't have enough movement in your low back to move *into* an anterior pelvic tilt, there's a good chance your low back feels stiff or achy.

So why has my client been told by well-meaning physical therapists and fitness professionals that her anterior pelvic tilt is a problem?

The first time I was exposed to the idea that anterior pelvic tilt was an issue was in Mabel Elsworth Todd's book *The Thinking Body*. I read it 15 years ago when I was first learning about somatics, a term used to describe bodywork and movement techniques that emphasize internal sensations, perceptions, and experiences of the body.

One of the exercises Todd suggests is to imagine you have a dinosaur tail while keeping the front of the body upright. I'm a good student, and I like to try out things, so for weeks I walked around pretending I had a dinosaur tail pulling the back of my pelvis down. The result? My pelvis tilted backward, reducing its natural movement, and I developed discomfort all through my lower back. As soon as I stopped trying to "fix" myself, the pain went away.

Maybe you would interpret this exercise differently than I did and not pull your pelvis so aggressively downward, which I don't actually think was Todd's intent (I tend to overdo things when I first learn about them). Or maybe you'd interpret it the same way but wouldn't feel discomfort. It's hard to know, because posture isn't a reliable indicator of whether someone will experience low back pain.

THE RISE OF THE "PELVIC TILT PROBLEM"

Visual assessments of pelvic position have been used in physical therapy clinics for decades. If the pelvis appeared tilted forward, the reasoning went, the muscles supporting it weren't in a biomechanically advantageous position to function properly. This was considered a problem. And when there is a problem, there is a diagnosis. In this case, the diagnosis was *anterior pelvic tilt*.

It wasn't long before certifications and continuing education courses emerged on how to *correct* anterior pelvic tilt so that clients and students could avoid this supposed dysfunction. Anterior pelvic tilt, apparently, was so bad it must be fixed before terrible things ensued.

WHAT THE RESEARCH ACTUALLY SAYS

Except—no one could agree on how much anterior pelvic tilt was actually a problem. And more curiously, researchers began finding that it wasn't the degree of tilt that mattered, but rather an overall *reduction* in low back movement.

So what were the fitness, movement, and rehab professions supposed to do if there wasn't a clear, visual way to define function versus dysfunction in the low back?

Some professionals clung to the idea, continuing to tell people that an anterior (or posterior) pelvic tilt was sure to give them low back pain. As the messaging persisted, people became scared to move their backs, afraid that moving "the wrong way" might cause irreparable harm. For some, that fear, combined with chronic clenching, bracing, and overcorrection, made things worse.

MOVEMENT, NOT POSTURE, IS WHAT MATTERS

Here's the thing: as you go about daily life bending, reaching, stooping, and turning—your spine *responds* to movement of your arms and legs by moving. It isn't a rigid structure. In fact, one of the most consistent findings in research on people with low back pain is that they tend to have *decreased range of motion and slower spinal movement* than people without low back pain. Posture is simply a temporary resting place. *Movement*, specifically how the joints coordinate and which joints are involved, carries far more meaning and weight in terms of how you move and how you feel.

PELVIC POSITION IN MOTION: ATHLETES AS EXAMPLES

Have you ever watched footage of **Sha'Carri Richardson** sprinting? Her pelvis is tipped forward, legs cycling powerfully behind her, and her spine rotates with each stride. The rapid movement of her limbs tugs at her spine, which responds dynamically by rotating. There is absolutely nothing wrong with her spine—in fact, trying to "fix" her anterior pelvic tilt would likely *reduce* her performance.

Conversely, if you watch the 2021 women's world record holder in the clean and jerk, Li Wenwen, lift, you'll see her pelvis tip backward and forward depending on the phase of the lift. As the weight moves, she moves around it, constantly adjusting her torso to navigate the shifting load.

The point is, the position of the pelvis is *relative* to how you're moving your torso. Is it going forward? Up? Down? Backward? To the right? To the left? Some combination of these? As long as movement in the lumbar spine is congruent with the direction of travel, your pelvis is moving exactly as it's supposed to.

WHEN THE PELVIS **STOPS MOVING**

The pelvis generally doesn't need to be micromanaged unless it:

a. doesn't move at all, or

b. moves in a way that isn't congruent with what's happening above or below it.

A pelvis that doesn't move is one that remains fixed in a single position regardless of activity. It's the pelvis that doesn't roll backward even when you're rounding your spine on the floor (and if you don't roll around on the ground, you totally should. It teaches you so much about softening through the spine). It's the pelvis that doesn't tip forward, making it difficult to lean your torso toward your thighs while sitting.

Whenever I ask someone who keeps their pelvis in a fixed position to move it, they are genuinely surprised by how *good* it feels. It's like the muscles of the low back have been in one position for so long, they have cobwebs. When they move, it's like they are beginning to clear the cobwebs out.

WHY THE PELVIS **GETS STUCK**

There are many reasons people lose pelvic movement. One of the main ones is that they've been taught their pelvis should stay still for spinal health. Other reasons include visual or vestibular challenges, cultural influences (like trying to appear smaller or bigger), protective patterns (common after sexual trauma or childbirth trauma), or injuries to the legs, feet, or spine.

Obviously, if any of those situations apply to you, it's important to seek appropriate help from a qualified medical provider.

HOW TO FREE THE ANUS (AND THE PELVIS)

But if you suspect you're someone who holds your pelvis rigidly because you were told not to move it, let's take a moment to talk about *how to free the anus*.

If your pelvis doesn't move, chances are high you're clenching somewhere. This is a generalization, but after years of observing clients, I've noticed a pattern:

- If you keep your pelvis tipped *forward* all the time, you tend to clench your abs.

- If you keep your pelvis tipped *backward* all the time, you tend to clench your glutes.

I once worked with a woman who kept her pelvis tipped backward **religiously because she'd been told in a small group class to do so for back health. She interpreted what the teacher said to mean that if she clenched both her abs and glutes she would protect her spine. She practiced the position so consistently that she trained her muscles to brace so much her spine didn't move and her low back hurt.*

HOW PELVIC POSITION INFLUENCES THE REST OF YOU

If you habitually hold your pelvis forward and never let it move backward, this affects what's happening in your ribs, jaw, and legs.

If you habitually hold your pelvis tucked backward and never let it move forward, you're also influencing what's occurring at the ribs, jaw, and legs.

Your pelvis is essentially the *center* of your body.* When you intentionally hold it in one position while moving, it impacts everything else. Let's look at this a little more closely.

**This is a generalization and is true for most people with two arms and two legs.*

EXPLORATION:
SITTING AWARENESS

TRY THIS:

Come into a seated position on a chair with your weight *in front* of your sitting bones (your sitting bones are the two pointy bones on the bottom of your pelvis that you can feel when you sit down).

Where are your ribs in relation to your pelvis? Are they forward, back, or shifted?

Now, roll your weight *behind* your sitting bones. Where are your ribs now?

Finally, sit *directly on top* of your sitting bones. Where are your ribs now?

REFLECTION

» What position feels most natural for you?

» What position feels most comfortable for you?

» Are the answers the same?

This simple seated exercise highlights how shifting the position of the pelvis often creates a shift in the position of the ribs—and we didn't even dive into weighting one side more than the other, or shifting one side of the pelvis forward or back.

Generally speaking, moving the pelvis will create a shift in what's happening at the ribs (unless you're trying to isolate movement at the pelvis—just watch a belly dancer or salsa dancer).

EXPLORATION: STANDING AWARENESS

> **TRY THIS:**
>
> Come into a standing position. Lock out your knees.

What happens to your pelvis? Does it move forward or back? Do you relax or tighten your glute muscles?

Now, relax your knees. What happens to your pelvis this time? Does it move forward or back? Do you relax or tighten your glutes?

REFLECTION

» What position feels most natural for you?

» What position feels most comfortable for you?

» Are they the same?

WHY AWARENESS MATTERS

Just because you always do something a certain way doesn't mean it's the way that actually feels best in your body. Taking a few moments to notice how you're standing, sitting, or lying down—and exploring subtle movements within that position—can serve as a *micro shield*.

These short explorations do two things that are foundational to **Spinal Intelligence**:

1. They develop body awareness.

2. They cultivate mindfulness in movement.

Developing body awareness fills in your brain's map of what you look like and how you move. This improves coordination, confidence, and helps your brain feel more secure with the body you inhabit.

The result? More coordination, confidence, and security when you move.

SUBTLE MOVEMENT AND THE MIND–BODY CONNECTION

Subtle, nuanced movement isn't the only way to improve body awareness. Any type of skilled movement—lifting weights, practicing Pilates or Tai Chi, training Parkour, or dancing—enhances awareness.

A subtle approach, though, is like using a finely sharpened colored pencil to add just the right amount of shading to a drawing. The picture would still look complete without it, but the shading brings it to life.

Modalities like **Tai Chi, yoga,** and **Pilates** utilize slow, internally focused approaches to movement and are often labeled "mind-body" disciplines. But when you look at what it means to be *mindful,* it becomes clear that any exercise can be a mind-body practice if it's approached with *openness* and *focus.*

Before we explore what I mean by those two qualities, it's worth noting that yoga, Pilates, and Tai Chi are excellent ways to slow down. This has immense value, and these practices can serve as *mini shields.*

However, if your movement practice consists *only* of slow, controlled movements, your internal awareness picture will miss some of the finer details about your body. Conversely, if you *only* practice fast, dynamic movement, you'll miss other shades of awareness that bring the full picture into focus.

MINI SHIELDS AND THE CONTINUUM OF MOVEMENT

Mini shields provide extra protection against life's physical and mental insults, but only when they're used in *conjunction* with your main shields, not as replacements.

Your daily movement exists on a continuum of fast and slow, thoughtful and automatic. Your movement practice should reflect that same continuum: include things that are fast and things that are slow; things that require deep focus and things you can do without overthinking.

I teach movement for a living, which means I also *practice* a lot of movement. I have my main shields, like strength training a couple of times a week and running four times a week. I also have my movement hobbies, which contain multiple shields and micro shields.

In my hobbies, I'm part of a supportive group. I'm learning something new regularly. I'm required to be present and mindful because I'm challenged, but not so challenged that it becomes anxiety-provoking. There's just enough risk to keep me engaged.

My movement hobbies include moments where I move quickly and moments where I move slowly. If you have a movement hobby, there's a good chance it includes both as well. Just like in life.

Spinal intelligence is the ability to move along these continuums, oscillating between strong and soft, slow and fast, and everything in between.

SELF-REFLECTION: THE SPEED YOU MOVE THROUGH LIFE

» Do you prefer to move fast or slow?

» What happens when you move fast? What happens when you move slow?

» Are there moments in your life where you have to move at a speed that doesn't feel comfortable to you?

Both moving fast and moving slowly require focus. Moving at a speed that's outside your comfort zone might initially feel awkward, anxiety-provoking, or irritating—but it might also feel surprisingly good.

Slow movement isn't necessarily easy movement, and fast movement isn't necessarily hard. When you move slowly, your brain has more time to register what you're feeling and what you're doing.

Try the examples below and notice what you experience.

EXPLORATION: THE SPEED CONTINUUM

Slow, hard movement:

Begin in a standing position. Squat down as slowly as you can. Imagine someone is pressing down on you as you descend.

Fast, easy movement:

Begin in a standing position with your knees slightly bent. Bounce up and down lightly, as if you're staying loose before a big athletic event.

Slow, easy movement:

Begin lying on the floor. Roll onto your right side as slowly and smoothly as possible. Pause. Then roll back onto your back, again as slowly and easily as possible.

Fast, hard movement:

Begin standing. Squat down and up as fast as you can ten times. If it feels comfortable, add a small jump as you rise from each squat.

REFLECTION

» Which style of movement did you like best?

» Which did you like least?

» Are there moments in your life where you could use more speed?

» Are there moments where you could use less?

» Did you feel focused while moving through these exercises, or did your mind wander?

OBSERVATION AND FOCUS:
THE HEADS AND TAILS OF MINDFULNESS

When you think of the word *mindfulness*, what comes to mind?

Maybe jot down a few ideas. No rush, I'll wait.

Mindfulness means being conscious or aware. It's both a *quality* and a *state*, but most importantly, it's an awareness of *right now*.

If you're thinking about the work call you just had with a co-worker, and you're *aware* that you're thinking about it, you're practicing mindfulness. If you're thinking about the call and your mind is spinning without awareness, you're *not* practicing mindfulness.

THE MINDFULNESS CONTINUUM

There are parts of daily life that demand awareness and parts that allow the brain to rest.

Just as movement exists on a continuum between fast and slow, mindfulness exists on a continuum between *attention* and *absence of* attention.

Cultivating both, and being able to recognize which state you're in, is a shield. Mindfulness can strengthen other shields when it's applied in the right dosage.

THE TWO MAIN ASPECTS OF AWARENESS

There are two aspects of awareness I'll discuss here. They aren't the only ones, but they're the most relevant to **Spinal Intelligence**.

If you're *aware* of something, you notice it. Noticing isn't labeling, judging, or creating a narrative around what it is or why it's there—it's simply *observation*.

THE BRAIN NETWORKS
BEHIND AWARENESS

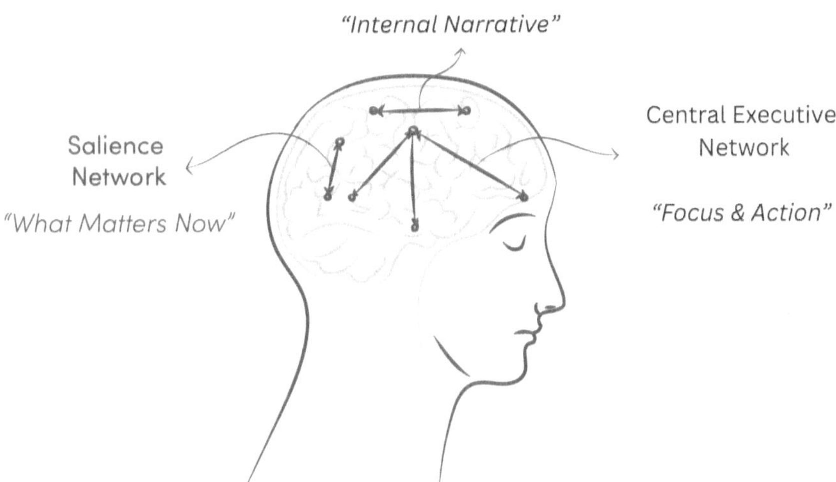

There are several networks in the brain that allow you to produce conscious thought. These networks are made up of different regions that work together so you can think, reason, and remember.

The internal voice many of us have running in the background most of the time is generated by the **default mode network**. You can think of this as the "voice inside your head."

When you practice open monitoring, you turn down the volume on the default mode network and turn up the volume on another system: the **salience network**.

The salience network helps you perceive the world around and within you. It determines what information is *salient*, or most important to pay attention to.

When the salience network's "volume" is turned too far *down* and can't be adjusted back up, it can lead to problems with understanding social cues, finding motivation, or experiencing pleasure.

On the other hand, a salience network that's turned too far *up* can cause you to pay excessive attention to certain stimuli, leading to a kind of hyper-vigilance.

FINDING THE RIGHT VOLUME

Have you ever stubbed your second toe? If you have, you know that this body part you don't ever think about can demand your full attention when it hurts because pain is loud.

But once you start doing something else, like playing with your dog or replying to your accountant about how many miles you drove this year for work, you forget about your toe. At least until you get up and try and walk, at which point you are quickly reminded that your middle toe still hurts.

That internal noise of your toe feeling sensation is your salience network at work, dialing your awareness of your middle toe up and down depending on what you are doing.

Now imagine you stub your middle toe, and hours later, while trying to write a paper, you can't stop thinking about it. You notice every sensation, every bit of pressure, and are completely unable to redirect your focus. Your salience network is no longer responding appropriately, dialing your internal awareness up and down. It has become mildly hysterical, has no volume knob, and is yelling at you unnecessarily.

An out of balance salience network can wreak havoc on your internal awareness. This happens in people with PTSD, anxiety, and chronic pain—the broken volume knob makes every sensation a potential threat that commands your attention and doesn't let it go.

The ability to adjust the "volume" between different brain networks is what allows mindfulness to function as a shield. When that adjustment mechanism stops working properly and you can't turn one down and turn another up, the system becomes unbalanced. The shield stops acting like a shield and becomes an *insult*.

THE BALANCE OF SHIELDS

This is the tricky part about maximizing the benefits of your shields: they only work well when used *holistically*.

If the balance between shields tips too far in one direction or if only one facet of a shield is used, it becomes easier for the system to be penetrated. Eventually, the very thing that was protecting you and giving you superpowers becomes potentially detrimental.

THE ROLE OF ATTENTION
IN LEARNING AND ADAPTATION

When you're learning something new, whether it's an exercise, a dance step, or a new language, you have to pay attention in order to actually learn.

In fact, many things in life benefit from sustained attention. Writing this book, for example, requires me to stay focused long enough to translate what's in my brain onto the page in a way that makes sense to someone else (even if that someone else is me).

FOCUSED ATTENTION AND THE CENTRAL EXECUTIVE NETWORK

As I was writing this passage, Nona, my uncannily aware dog, appeared, looking for attention. She dislikes it when my focus isn't entirely on her, so she wedged herself between me and the computer until I stopped what I was doing, and gave her the pets she wanted. Once she was satisfied, I told her to lie down and returned to writing.

The **salience network** is what allowed me to see her in my peripheral vision and notice when she started nudging the computer (which, admittedly, was hard to miss). The **central executive network** is what allowed me to put the computer down and direct my attention fully toward her.

When I saw through her body language that she was content, my salience network registered the cue, and my central executive network helped me shift my attention back to the words on the screen.

Your **central executive network** is the brain network that helps you perform cognitive tasks that require focus—things like sustaining attention, inhibiting impulses, identifying relevant cues, following directions, and problem-solving.

EVERYDAY EXAMPLES OF COGNITIVE COORDINATION

Imagine it's a Wednesday. You're about to leave work when you get a text from your best friend: they've scored a reservation at the new restaurant in town for 8:00 p.m. You'd have to skip the gym to go, and you have a big project due by the end of the week.

If your central executive network is functioning well, you pause, weigh your options, and decide to decline—this is *inhibition*.

If you go to the gym and stay present while learning a new exercise or completing your sets and reps without checking your phone, that's your central executive network helping you maintain focus and attention.

And if, the next morning, you sit down at work, check your email once, silence your notifications, and dedicate an hour to uninterrupted deep work—again, that's your central executive network in action.

COORDINATION BETWEEN NETWORKS

While the central executive network plays a crucial role in attention and control, what matters even more is the *ability to fluidly shift* between brain networks.

If you can't coordinate between the **default mode network** (your background mental chatter) and the **central executive network** (your task-focused system), you may be more prone to anxiety. Similarly, children with ADHD often struggle to coordinate all three networks—the default mode, salience, and central executive networks.

I haven't talked much about coordination yet, but know this: **coordination is the key to movement freedom**, so it's not surprising that it's also key to a healthy mind.

Practicing mindfulness in everyday life helps you toggle more easily between these networks. It influences how you *feel*, how you *communicate*, and how you *move*.

THE MIND, THE BODY, AND POSTURE

So what does all of this have to do with posture and anterior pelvic tilt?

Any time you try to control every aspect of your movement, you create an imbalance between these brain networks. This can reinforce the idea that the body and mind are separate, that the body can't be trusted to keep itself safe, and that the mind must take over.

But the body, like the brain, produces movement through a series of *coordinations*. (And to be clear, that series of coordinations is determined by the brain and the spinal cord in response to the inputs it's receiving at that exact moment.) Overemphasizing one area, like the pelvis, interrupts this natural coordination.

Let's say you were driving to pick up a friend to go to a concert. You always take a specific route to their house, so you begin driving. You notice detour signs, but you ignore them because this is the route you take to get to where you are going.

Ten minutes later, you are sitting at a standstill. The road is completely blocked and you can't get through. Everything is locked up because you ignored the signals from the environment that you should go a different direction.

When you try to hold a body part a particular way every time you move, eventually you will find yourself at a standstill. The brain uses lots of information (input) to determine the best way to coordinate the desired movement. Rather than trying to control the output, or the movement, you are a lot better off manipulating the inputs.

As you learned earlier, the position of the pelvis depends on what's happening *above* it and *below* it. Many movement modalities that focus on strengthening the torso understand this intuitively: the position of the rib cage relative to the pelvis, the arms relative to the ribs, and the legs relative to the feet all influence what you experience in your so-called "core."

PRACTICING SPINAL INTELLIGENCE

Practicing **Spinal Intelligence** means focusing on movement and task efficiency from a place of curiosity. You don't have to obsess over a specific posture because with the right input, *your posture will change*.

This is what happens when you build balanced strength, develop total-body coordination, and explore a wide variety of movement patterns.

WHAT COMES NEXT

What happens if you experience pain or discomfort and aren't sure where to start?

Stay tuned—that's what we'll explore next.

BRINGING IT ALL TOGETHER:
MINDFULNESS IN MOTION

Before we move on, try the explorations below.

How does applying mindfulness change your experience?

MINDFULNESS EXERCISE 1:
THE SQUAT – OPEN MONITORING

Begin:

Start standing. Imagine you have a tail and gently move it forward and backward.

Find a place where it feels like your "tail" is *free*.

From there, reach the underside of your booty toward the floor. Move slowly enough that you can observe what happens—if it doesn't feel like the underside of your booty reaching down, simply notice that.

When you reach a natural stopping point, stand back up. Perform this one or two times.

Next:

The next time you lower down, observe what happens in your torso.

- Do your ribs rotate forward?

- Do they move backward?

- Do they stay still?

Try squatting two or three times with your ribs in *different* positions.

- What feels easiest?

- What feels hardest?

- What feels most natural?

Now, look at your feet.

- How far apart are they?

- Do they rotate inward, outward, or point straight ahead?

Squat again—two to four times—with your feet in different positions.

Move slowly. Notice:

- What feels most comfortable?

- Where do you feel the most space?

- Is that how you usually squat?

THE SQUAT – FOCUSED ATTENTION

For this variation, you'll need a small ball that you can toss.

Begin:

Start standing. Toss the ball gently into the air.

Catch it as you squat down. Repeat this two or three times.

Next:

On your next round, toss the ball up *while you're in the squat* and catch it as you stand up. Repeat two or three times.

REFLECTION

- » Which of these squat variations emphasized the salience network?

- » Which emphasized the central executive network?

- » Which version did you prefer—and why?

THE TAKEAWAY

Mindfulness in movement isn't about perfect form or controlling every detail.

It's about noticing—where your attention goes, how your body responds, and what feels natural.

When you bring awareness to even simple actions, like a squat, you strengthen the connection between your body and mind, train your nervous system to adapt, and expand your capacity for movement freedom.

That's the essence of Spinal Intelligence—cultivating awareness of how your spine participates and having confidence that your central nervous system knows what it's doing and can coordinate what it's doing as you move.

REFLECTION: CHAPTER 5 – COORDINATION, MINDFULNESS, AND THE MOVING PELVIS

Your pelvis, spine, and brain all work together through coordination. When one part of the system becomes rigid—whether it's a physical structure like the pelvis or a mental structure like attention—the entire system loses flexibility.

Mindfulness, curiosity, and awareness restore balance. The goal isn't to perfect posture or eliminate movement patterns—it's to notice, to explore, and to find a dynamic relationship between awareness and action.

When you shift your focus from "fixing" to *feeling*, from "alignment" to *coordination*, you begin to move with greater ease, efficiency, and trust in your body's intelligence.

REFLECTION PROMPTS

- What did you notice about your pelvis and ribs as you experimented with different sitting, standing, and squatting positions?

- How does moving with open monitoring (noticing without judgment) feel different from moving with focused attention (directed awareness)?

- Do you tend to hold tension in specific areas—like your abs, glutes, or jaw—when you're trying to control movement?

- How does that tension change when you bring mindful curiosity to the movement instead?

- In your daily life, where might you be over-managing movement or attention—and where could you invite more freedom and trust?

INTEGRATION

This week, choose one everyday movement—standing up from a chair, reaching for something, walking—and practice it with awareness. Notice your breath, your weight shift, and the rhythm of your movement.

See what happens when you let the body guide the mind, rather than the other way around.

That's the beginning of *spinal intelligence in motion.*

CHAPTER 6:
THE MYTH OF THE CORE

"I need to strengthen my core."

Over the last 23 years, I've heard this countless times when talking with new clients about their goals. The *core*, it seems, has been placed on a pedestal—as if, when properly strengthened and "activated," it will solve all problems, including (but not limited to) back pain, urinary incontinence, sagging skin, and your teenage daughter's boyfriend.

I jest, but in all seriousness, there's a deeply ingrained belief that *core strength is king*.

But what exactly is *core strength*? Or *core activation*? Or *core anything*? And is one type of core strength better than another? Why does it matter so much?

THE FEAR OF BACK PAIN

Human beings are understandably afraid of injuring their backs. Nearly everyone knows someone who has experienced back pain. In fact, according to the Bureau of Labor Statistics, of 349,050 work-related injuries in 2016, 134,550 were related to the back. For those of you who are into statistics, that equates to **38.5%** of all reported work injuries.

A large percentage of those work injuries occurred among nursing assistants and laborers, but they aren't the only ones getting low back pain. When you look at the general population, it's estimated that **80% of adults** will experience back pain at some point in their lives, and at this exact moment, **1 in 4** adults has low back pain. Most of the time, it resolves on its own within 3 months, but sometimes it doesn't. For some people, it persists and becomes chronic.

What it means for low back pain to be chronic is tricky. Researchers don't have a uniform way to measure chronic, and people who seek medical care for low back pain excludes people who never go to the doctor but still have low back pain. Some of those individuals seek alternative forms of care and take a holistic approach, and some, when they find something that finally works, they become evangelists for the practitioner or technique.

So yes—back pain is real and prevalent. But let's take a closer look at *why*.

THE WEIGHT OF WORK

Some professions inherently carry a higher risk of low back injury. Take, for instance, nursing assistants. Their daily responsibilities include making beds, bathing patients, and transporting people who may not be able to assist in their own movement.

My dad has been in a skilled nursing facility for over two and a half years after a massive stroke left him paralyzed on his left side. One of his favorite things is going for car rides.

A year ago, I rented a mid-sized SUV and, with the help of a nursing assistant, tried to get him into the car. My dad is a large man—6'1" and about 200 pounds. I am 5'1", 125 pounds, so there is a minor size discrepancy. The nursing assistant who helped me was taller than I am and sturdy. When we tried to help my dad move from his wheelchair to the car, due to his disability, he couldn't help us by pushing through his feet.

We tried to lift him, but he fell sideways into the car. He didn't have the strength to get onto the seat and the angle was awkward for us to try and help maneuver him. After several attempts, we finally got him back into his wheelchair. We didn't take the drive that day. Now, we use a car service that can wheel his chair directly into a van.

Two hundred pounds of deadweight is very different from two hundred pounds of someone who can help move themselves. It's awkward. You're worried about hurting them—which means you're not paying attention to what's happening in *your own* body.

I learned quickly that lifting him wasn't a good choice for me. But nursing assistants do this kind of lifting, along with bathing and repositioning patients, *every day*. Add in the repetitive strain of making beds and handling equipment, and it's no wonder low back pain is a frequent occurrence.

Any one of these tasks, done occasionally, is totally fine. If you have a baseline of general strength, you can probably do these tasks more than occasionally. But if you were to do all of these tasks, day after day, year after year, the physical stress begins to outweigh the body's ability to adapt, especially if the person inhabiting that body is having trouble sleeping, has stress in their personal life, or doesn't have a good physical and emotional support system.

WHY SOME BACKS HURT MORE THAN OTHERS

So yes—some professions naturally carry a higher likelihood of back pain because of the physical nature of the work. But most low back pain, about **85–90%**, is *non-specific*, meaning there's no clear structural cause. And, I know I said this just a moment ago, but I will say it again, most of it resolves within three months, regardless of treatment.

Chronic pain, however, is a different story. It's exhausting, emotionally and physically. It can make people short-tempered, anxious, and fearful that life will never feel "normal" again.

If you have chronic lower back pain that doesn't have a structural cause, you can train your core until the cows come home, the chances of a full resolution may be slim without a holistic approach.

WHEN EXERCISE BECOMES A SHIELD

Sometimes, people find relief in a specific exercise modality, often one with a charismatic, confident leader who insists they have *the answer*. These systems can be appealing because they offer structure, precision, and certainty.

Leaders of these programs often extend their advice beyond movement. They educate on things like nutrition, inflammation, and lifestyle, all with the same conviction they use to explain why their exercises are superior (and usually with fewer qualifications).

This can be empowering for some people, but problematic for others.

Many individuals with chronic pain feel unseen or unheard by the medical system. They search for answers, traveling from one specialist to another. Unless they end up in the care of a pain specialist, many physicians don't have the time to delve into all the different factors that contribute to chronic pain.*

Pro tip—if you are struggling with chronic pain and you aren't sleeping, tell your doctor both of those things. Primary care physicians take insomnia seriously.

Traditional exercise programs often fail them because, even when they report flare-ups, the coach doesn't know how to adjust or offer alternatives. This isn't the coach's fault—they are taught how to create progressive exercise programs, not how to deal with flare-ups.

But when these individuals find a system that begins with **non-threatening movement**, allows them to build **exercise tolerance** gradually, and is guided by a **supportive coach,** often, something shifts.

Instead of exercise being an *insult* to the system, it becomes a **shield**.

And once it becomes a shield, it's like the nervous system is given an opening to finally shift a different direction.

WHAT THE "BEST" SYSTEM
HAS IN COMMON

When people ask me which type of exercise is best for low back pain, my answer is always the same: *Yes.*

Because most forms of movement can be helpful when offered thoughtfully and approached through non-threatening movement first, followed by movements that develop trust in the physical structure, followed by strength and more dynamic forms of movement.

Effective systems usually share certain principles:

- They initially involve some type of body awareness, whether it's foam rolling/self myofascial release, gentle awareness drills, gentle mobility drills, like joint circles.

- They start with simple, often isometric exercises in supported positions.

- They emphasize **breathing** and internal awareness.

- They progress **gradually**, introducing load and weight shifting as tolerance improves.

- They eventually move into multi-rotational, **dynamic** movement, that is both challenging and mentally engaging.

THE PROBLEM WITH "FIXING"

Many of these programs describe their exercises as *corrective*—targeting perceived dysfunctions like muscle imbalances, pelvic misalignment, or "improper" firing patterns.

These narratives often work because they give structure and meaning to movement, but they also carry a hidden cost: they reinforce the idea that something is *wrong* with the body.

This can be disempowering, and it creates unnecessary competition between movement modalities. On social media, thought leaders in the corrective and functional exercise space often explain why their approach is better than Mr. A's approach. Mr. A responds that the modality Mr. B teaches isn't doing anything and obviously, Mr. B is selling snake oil, even though Mr. B legitimately has hundreds of testimonials. The arguments over whose approach is "the best" or "most corrective," for the average person scrolling through social media trying to find good information, are confusing at best and overwhelming at worst.

WHAT I'VE SEEN WORK

I've seen many things work.

I've watched posture shift before my eyes when someone is invited to move differently.

I know three people who resolved their chronic low back pain simply by falling—accidentally—on the opposite side of their pain (not a recommended intervention, but fascinating nonetheless).

I've led workshops where a single breathing exercise relieved a woman's mid-back pain she'd had for years.

And I've had clients whose chronic low back pain began to ease after just two sessions.

But I've also had clients for whom my work didn't resonate—and who found success elsewhere.

That's the point: *different systems work for different people.*

THE ROLE OF THE MOVEMENT PROFESSIONAL

A movement coach isn't a pain specialist. Our job isn't to treat pain—it's to guide people toward strength, awareness, and efficiency.

And yet, people in pain frequently seek guidance from movement professionals. At this point, I generally have a really good idea of what to do if someone walks in with chronic low back pain and it doesn't involve promising I am going to fix anything. If you have chronic low back pain, unless you're working directly with a physiotherapist or rehab professional, movement isn't a tool to fix you. It's a process to help you reconnect with your body and move forward.

When exercise is approached from that perspective—*meeting you where you are*—it becomes one of the most powerful shields we have.

THE EVOLUTION OF "CORE STRENGTH"

How does all of this relate to core weakness and core strength?

The idea that the core could be weak has a long history.

THE MODERN ERA OF CORE TRAINING

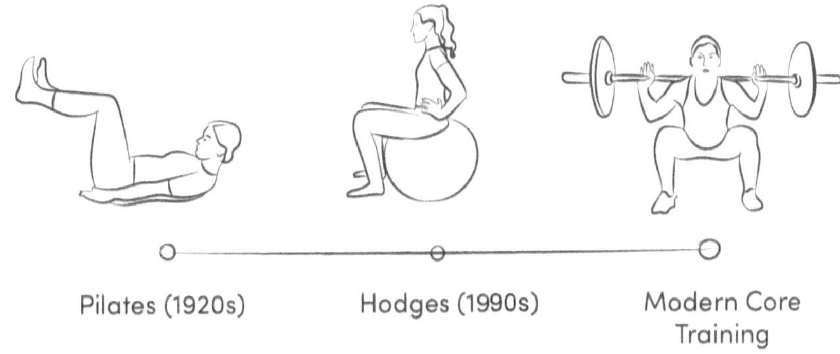

In the early 20th century, a German-born civilian named Joseph Pilates was interned in England during WWI. He used his time in the internment camps to develop a system of exercises aimed at improving the physical and mental condition of the men around him. In 1926, he migrated from Germany to New York City and opened a studio, initially working with dancers. Word of his work spread, and eventually, he attracted a diverse clientele.

Pilates, both the man and his method, is often considered synonymous with the advent of core training. He called his method contrology and it was designed to unify the mind, body, and spirit. The exercises focused on precision and were designed to be executed a specific way, through breath, concentration, centering, control, and flow. The term centering referred to movement coming from the center of the body; later teachers coined this "the powerhouse."

While Pilates certainly wasn't the first person to focus on the abdominals as a foundation for movement, he is, perhaps, the first well-known proselytizer of the core in all of its proverbial glory.

THE RESEARCH ERA: THE 1990S AND BEYOND

Seventy years later, Pilates began to emerge as a trending fitness modality right as researcher Paul Hodges and his team were publishing a series of studies on the role of the *transverse abdominis* in posture and movement.

Some of those early studies examined *timing*—when the transverse abdominis fired during movement.

Others looked at posture and how the transverse abdominis supported posture. One highly frequently cited paper during that era examined the role of the *diaphragm* in postural stability. (The diaphragm, conveniently for Pilates, is a breathing muscle you have some voluntary control over. This means you can alter how and when you breathe, unlike other autonomic functions—you can't exactly tell the bile when to secrete bile.)

What many professionals took away from Hodges's body of work was that the spine is inherently unstable when the transverse abdominis isn't firing properly. The narrative became that when the deep core muscles properly coordinate, they create a degree of stiffness that enhances stability.

Before you embrace the idea that there is anything wrong with your transverse abdominis, there are some important caveats:

- Many of these studies were conducted with very small sample sizes.

- Some used *pig spines*, not human subjects.

- When comparing timing of muscle activation, researchers often studied people with chronic low back pain and compared them to pain-free individuals. If something hurts, you move differently, so comparing muscle activation timing between these groups is a little bit like comparing apples and oranges.

While these studies weren't the only research influencing the idea that the core is central to spinal health, they were frequently cited as justification for "weak cores," "strong cores," and why everyone supposedly needed core-specific exercises. (If you were around during this era, you might remember the blood pressure cuff and its role in teaching one of the most tedious core exercises ever.)

DOES THE CORE MATTER?

Of course it does. *All of you matters*.

But is the core *more important* to train than other areas? Not necessarily. The era of core stability as king persisted far longer than it should have, but fortunately a more balanced narrative is beginning to emerge.

Here's the thing about your core—if you're moving, it's moving. The more complex or physically demanding your movements become, the more your core participates, because you're not a collection of isolated parts—you're a *system*.

That said, targeted work for the muscles supporting the spine can absolutely be beneficial—but maybe not for the reasons most people assume.

REBUILDING
THE INTERNAL BODY MAP

Earlier, I mentioned that your **internal body map** is how your body is represented in your brain. This representation is both conscious and unconscious, shaped by what you can *see* and what you can *feel*, and it's closely related to movement.

When you injure an area, have surgery, or simply stop moving a region of your body, that internal map becomes disrupted.

Because body representation is based on sensory input—what you see and feel—you can use both as tools to *reconnect* with your body. This process is powerful for managing pain and rebuilding confidence and resilience. It's a kind of *under armor*. You can think of it as a **primary shield**.

Targeted core work helps you reconnect with the center of your body, just as massage or self-myofascial release can help you sense different body parts. It's like your brain saying, "Ah, there I am."

It feels good—your body feels *awake, coordinated, and alive with sensation* (and who doesn't want that?).

BUILDING A POSITIVE FEEDBACK LOOP

All of this reconnecting with your body through concentrated movement creates a positive feedback loop that looks like this:

You feel stronger and more confident → You move more and in new ways → You continue to strengthen the connection between your brain and body.

If your internal body map has become "fuzzy" because of pain, inactivity, or surgery, you'll naturally avoid using that area. Spending time exploring positions and movements you've neglected becomes an entry point to improving your **body representation** and **proprioception** (your unconscious awareness of where you are in space, based on sensory input like pressure and touch).

SO... IS CORE TRAINING BETTER THAN GENERAL EXERCISE?

I know, I know. I keep asking the question and I haven't exactly answered it. That's because honestly? We don't know—and goodness, does the internet love to argue about it.

Here's what I do know: for a lot of people, **core awareness feels good**.

I also know that any exercise can be a core exercise. If you like doing core-specific exercises, do them. But if that's *all* you do, you're missing out on the benefits of total-body strength and coordination.

It's worth remembering that one of the original uses of **Pilates** in the United States was as a supplemental training method for **dancers**. The *training* itself—the art, the dance—was always the main event.

REDEFINING THE CORE

Before we move on, take a moment to reflect.

Write down three exercises you commonly think of as core exercises.

1. ____

2. ____

3. ____

What about these makes them core exercises?

Now, **write down three exercises you think of as basic exercises.**

1. ____

2. ____

3. ____

How could you make these basic exercises *feel* more like core exercises?
And—perhaps more importantly—is that even necessary?

MY EXAMPLES

Here are some of the examples I came up with off the top of my head:

Three exercises I think of as core exercises:

- Hands-on-blocks plank position, alternating hands on blocks

- Candlestick

- Goblet squat with a pulse and a focus on breath

I think of these as core exercises because I *feel* them in my abdominals.

Three exercises I think of as basic exercises:

- Split-stance squats

- Push-ups

- Bodyweight rows (using rings or stall bars)

Interestingly, this list was more challenging than I expected. It turns out my brain doesn't naturally categorize movements into "core" or "basic."

MAKING IT FEEL LIKE THE CORE

If I wanted to make these basic exercises *feel* more like core exercises—that is, if I wanted to increase my sense of core engagement—I could:

- Add a **focused breath**

- Start low and stay low, or pay attention to an **internal shift** in my abdominals as I step

- Bring awareness to the **relationship between my rib cage and pelvis**

Would it be *necessary* to turn these into core-focused exercises? Not really.

However, it might be a valuable experiment if:

- You feel like your core is a deep, black hole you can't sense

- You experience negative sensations or discomfort in your low back

- You're working to improve body awareness for a specific activity—like aerial silks, rope, or static pole

(And yes—you'll find all of these exercises explained at the end of the chapter.)

Otherwise, there's probably no need to overthink it.

THE ELUSIVE DEFINITION OF "CORE"

I've said this before, but it bears repeating: **one of the biggest issues with the idea of a "core exercise" is that there's no universal definition of what the core actually is.**

If pressed, I might define the core as "any of the muscles that attach to the spine."

But that definition leaves out the **pelvic floor**, which doesn't seem right—so perhaps it's "any of the muscles that attach to the spine *and* the pelvic floor."

Yet that definition excludes the muscles that stabilize the **outside of the pelvis**, which feels incomplete.

So if I expand the definition again, suddenly I'm including everything from the **shoulders to the hips.**

And maybe that's closer to the truth.

THE MYTHICAL CORE

The core has been inflated into something mythical—an area that, when strengthened, will supposedly protect you from harm, prevent injury, improve posture, and grant a kind of physical invincibility.

But the truth is simpler and more empowering:

The core isn't a single thing you can isolate or "fix." It's a **dynamic relationship** between your spine, pelvis, breath, and awareness—a coordination that reflects how *you* move.

I've known strength and conditioning coaches with low back pain.

I've also known Pilates teachers and biomechanics professors—experts who specialize in studying the back—who have back pain.

Just like strength isn't a cure-all but rather a **shield** that works with other shields to create resiliency, targeted core work isn't an armor. It's a **mini-shield**—one that can contribute to pain-free movement when it's integrated with the rest of the system.

THE POWER OF ASYMMETRY

In 2002, a fifteen-year-old from rural Jamaica stepped to the starting blocks at the World Junior Championships in Track and Field, in front of 36,000 spectators. He won the gold medal in the 200 meters.

Six years later, he would set a record in the 100 meters that still stands—**9.58 seconds**—despite having scoliosis (diagnosed in his early teens) and a right leg that was half an inch shorter than his left.

His name was **Usain Bolt**. Researchers suggest that one reason for his extraordinary speed was that he learned to use his natural asymmetry to his advantage.

Bolt's career wasn't injury-free. He began experiencing hamstring injuries during the 2004 World Junior Championships, and thirteen years later, dur-

---

ing what was to be his final professional race, he tore his left hamstring. While it's easy to assume the scoliosis was the cause of his hamstring issues, hamstring injuries can occur when you're running over **22 miles per hour**. They're rare, but once they happen, there's roughly a one-in-five chance of recurrence.

UNDERSTANDING SCOLIOSIS

The word *scoliosis* comes from the Greek *skolios*, meaning *curved* or *crooked*. It describes a spine that curves like the letter C. There are several variations, and depending on the pattern, it can create visual asymmetries such as one shoulder sitting higher, ribs shifting, or the pelvis appearing elevated on one side.

As we've already discussed, posture is a *temporary* snapshot in time.

Scoliosis, however, is a structural variation of the skeleton. It's not actually that common—it only affects between **0.47% and 5.2%** of adolescents.

Adults have a higher rate of occurrence because of something called *primary degenerative scoliosis*. We'll break down what that means in a moment, but the estimated prevalence is wildly varied, ranging from **13%–68%**.

RETHINKING "DEGENERATIVE"

The term *degenerative* is misleading. It implies inevitable decline or irreversible damage. While that may be true for certain neurological conditions such as multiple sclerosis or ALS, the term is also applied to musculoskeletal issues like osteoarthritis, spinal stenosis, and adult-onset scoliosis.

In reality, many "degenerative" conditions can be improved. For example, treatments for early-stage osteoarthritis* can impact how it progresses and, in some cases, appear to halt it altogether.

*Osteoarthritis is inflammation of the tissues around the joint. It leads to cartilage breakdown and bone erosion, changing the structure of the joint. It's also the most common chronic musculoskeletal disorder.

Primary degenerative scoliosis is scoliosis that usually develops in the lumbar spine in people over the age of 50. It occurs when the facet joints (the joints on the back of the spine that link vertebrae together) and intervertebral discs degenerate. This type of scoliosis is often accompanied by osteoarthritis or osteoporosis.

Fortunately, this type of scoliosis responds well to conservative treatment. Recent studies found that adults with scoliosis who participated in physical therapy and continued to exercise three times per week after treatment, experienced improved function, reduced pain, and enhanced quality of life.

Like the saying goes, movement is medicine.

There are some targeted exercise treatments for different types of scoliosis. One that appears to be particularly effective is the **Schroth Method**. The Schroth Method is a movement-based approach designed specifically for scoliosis. People with scoliosis who utilize the Schroth Method consistently demonstrate improvements in posture, function, and overall well-being.

I actually bought the book about the Schroth Method to learn more about it. It's a smart program—it utilizes breathing, isometric positions, and focused, mind-body exercises. Does that sound familiar?

This leads me all of the way back to my original query—how *degenerative* are some of these degenerative conditions, really?

PAIN, PERCEPTION, AND POSSIBILITY

There isn't always a clear answer, which is why it's important you seek medical advice if you are given the diagnosis of degenerative anything.

It's also worth remembering that people can have osteoarthritis, spinal stenosis (narrowing of the spinal canal) or scoliosis and experience *no pain* at all.

Others experience severe pain that resolves completely after surgery, and others have pain even after they have surgery.

Why do some people hurt while others don't?

I wish I knew the definitive answer.

What I *do* know is this: when your **main shields** are strong, your **durability** increases.

DURABILITY VS. RESILIENCE

Durability is your ability to withstand wear, pressure, or damage.

In the wellness world, we often glorify *resilience*—the ability to recover from misfortune or change (as defined by *Merriam-Webster*).

Recovery matters, of course, but I'd argue that **being able to withstand** challenges is even more essential.

Your **main shields** build durability.

Your **micro-shields** strengthen both durability and resilience.

REVISITING YOUR SHIELDS

I know there's only so much time in the day—and that life is constantly, well, *life-ing*.

But if you go back and review your list of shields from Chapter 2, remember: **it's not about duration—it's about consistency.**

A fifteen-minute run five times a week will do more for your durability than a single hour-long run once a week.

(Unless that hour-long run is with friends—in which case, the social connection from the friends might balance it out.)

STRENGTHENING SHIELDS AND MICRO-SHIELDS

If you haven't already, take a look back at your list from Chapter 2 and note which shields you checked.

Remember that each main shield can be supported by smaller **micro-shields**. Micro-shields are specific habits or strategies that make the bigger shield possible.

For example:

- **Main Shield:** Consistent sleep
  - **Micro-Shields:**
    - Put the phone away 45 minutes before bed
    - Read before falling asleep
  - Use mouth taping to encourage nasal breathing

- **Main Shield:** A fulfilling partnership (or cultivating social connection)

  - **Micro-Shields:**

    - Participate in a weekly activity you enjoy outside the home

    - Say yes to new experiences

    - Practice open communication with friends and coworkers

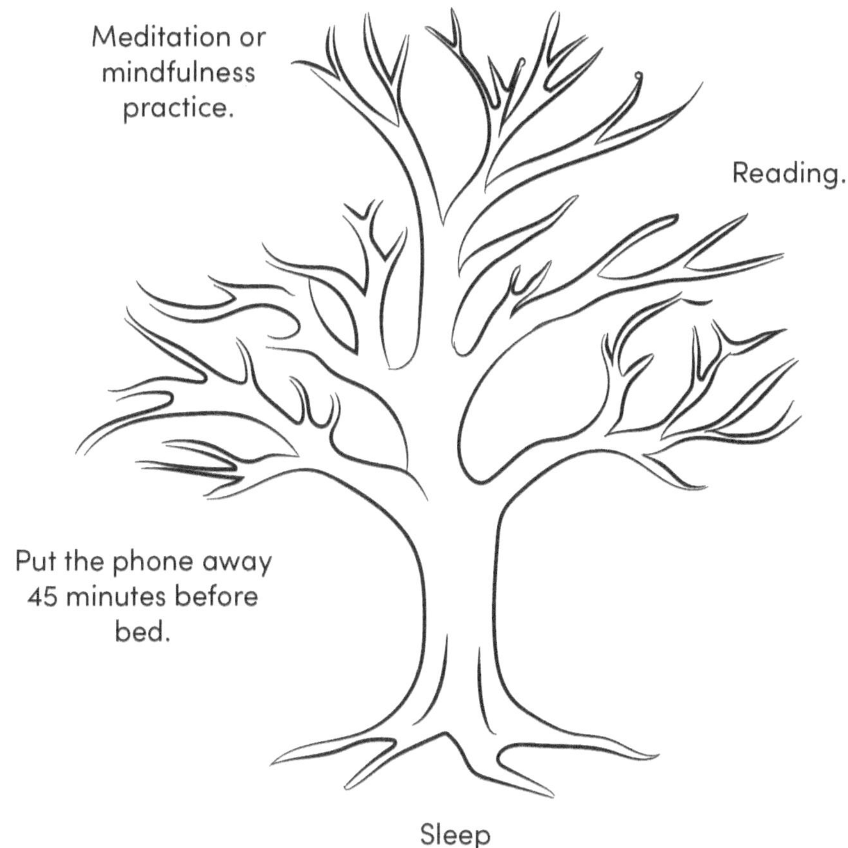

REFLECTION: STRENGTHENING YOUR SYSTEM

Take a moment to place a **checkmark (√)** next to two or three shields you'd like to improve or develop.

☐ A sense of community

☐ A fulfilling family life

☐ A partner or spouse

☐ Regular cardiovascular activity

☐ A fulfilling hobby

☐ A sense of purpose

☐ A regular meditation practice

☐ Consistent sleep

☐ Regularly learning new things

☐ Regularly consuming whole foods

☐ A creative outlet

☐ Regular time in nature

☐ Financial security

Now, write down **two or three micro-shields** for each one you selected—small, actionable habits or steps that can help you strengthen or move toward that shield.

____

____

____

____

(Example: if your shield is "Consistent sleep," your micro-shields might include putting your phone away 45 minutes before bed, reading before sleep, and keeping a consistent bedtime.)

PRACTICE:

Add *one* shield or micro-shield next week—the one that feels most accessible.

Afterward, write a single sentence about your experience.

Reflect:

- How did it go?

- How did it make you feel?

- Is it something worth repeating?

NEXT STEPS

Below are the **basic and core exercises** from earlier in the chapter, with brief descriptions.

After you try them, ask yourself:

- Where do I feel connected?

- Where do I feel energized?

PRACTICE: BASIC AND CORE EXERCISES

The practices and exercises below are a way to experience feeling supported by your spine as you move. Exercises like these tend to create a little heat through the muscles that are commonly thought of as core exercises. That heat translates into confidence—confidence that your spine is strong and supported when you move.

Use these explorations to connect awareness, breath, and coordination through your center. Move slowly, stay curious, and notice how each variation changes how you feel.

3 CORE EXERCISES

1. PLANK: ALTERNATING HANDS ON YOGA BLOCKS

Setup:

Begin either on hands and knees with your hands on yoga blocks, or in a plank position with your hands elevated on yoga blocks.

Movement:

1. Press one hand firmly into the yoga block as you lift the other hand off and place it on the floor.

2. Press the hand on the floor firmly down as you lift the opposite hand off the yoga block and place it on the floor.

3. Press one hand into the floor as you return the other hand to the yoga block.

4. Repeat, alternating hands, maintaining a steady breath.

Repetitions: 3–5 times.

2. CANDLESTICK

Setup:

Lie on your back with your arms by your sides. You may keep your knees bent with feet on the floor or extend your legs straight.

Movement:

1. Inhale to prepare.

2. Exhale and reach your legs straight toward the ceiling.

3. Press your arms into the floor and imagine your toes touching the ceiling as your hips lift and you roll slightly onto your upper back.

4. Inhale and slowly lower your legs back down.

Repetitions: 3–5 times.

3. **GOBLET SQUAT WITH PULSE AND FOCUSED BREATH**

Setup:

Stand holding a kettlebell (bottoms-up) or a dumbbell with both hands close to your chest. Keep your elbows by your sides.

Movement:

1. **Inhale** as you squat down.

2. **Exhale** and come up one-quarter of the way, making a small pulse.

3. **Inhale** to lower back down.

4. **Exhale** to stand all the way up.

Repetitions: 2–4 rounds.

3 BASIC EXERCISES
WITH A CORE-CENTERED FOCUS

I said earlier that any exercise can be a core-focused exercise. Here are some examples.

1. **SPLIT-STANCE SQUATS**

Setup:

Step your right foot forward. Let your torso lean slightly forward, as if you could crouch down at any moment.

Movement:

1. Imagine the skin beneath your belly button rotating left.

2. As you squat down, imagine that skin rotating right.

3. Return to standing and repeat.

Repetitions: 2–4 per side.

Options:

- Hold a weight with both hands.

- Hold a weight in the **right hand** (same side as front leg) either down by your side or in a rack position.

- Hold a weight in the **left hand** (opposite side) and reach it toward the inside of the front shin as you lower.

- Add a focused breath: *inhale down, exhale up.*

- Shift your awareness to the **pelvic floor** rotation: when the right leg is forward, begin with the pelvic floor rotating left; as you descend, rotate it right; rotate it back left as you rise.

2. PUSH-UPS

Setup:

Begin in a straight-arm push-up position. Knees may be on or off the floor, and hands may rest on the floor or elevated on yoga blocks.

Movement:

1. Imagine your hands **rotating outward** as you lower toward the floor—this helps you pull yourself down with control.

2. Imagine your hands **rotating inward** as you push away from the floor.

Options:

- Visualize a line between your **pubic symphysis** (front of pelvis) and your **xiphoid process** (base of sternum). Maintain that connection as you move.

- At the top, reach the xiphoid process and ribs gently toward the ceiling.

- Inhale into the space between the shoulder blades.

- Exhale as you lower yourself down.

3. BODYWEIGHT ROWS

Setup:

Hold rings, stall bars, a Smith-rack bar, or a suspension trainer. Lean back so your arms are straight.

Movement:

1. Wiggle slightly until you feel your ribs and pelvis connected.

2. Imagine a line from the **back of the armpit** to the **pinky finger.**

3. Use that line to pull the rings toward your chest.

4. Lower yourself back to the starting position with control.

Options:

- Use a focused breath:

    - Try inhaling as you lower and exhaling as you pull.

    - Then reverse: exhale as you lower, inhale as you pull. Which feels better?

- Change your position by moving farther underneath the rings.

- Try starting seated on the floor: bridge your hips up, pull, and lower down while keeping awareness of the **relationship between ribs and pelvis** throughout.

REFLECTION

After completing these exercises, pause and notice:

» Where do you feel **connected**?

» Where do you feel **energized**?

» How does awareness shift when you bring focused attention to your breath and core?

CHAPTER 7:
COMPRESSION, EXPANSION, AND THE FABRIC OF MOVEMENT

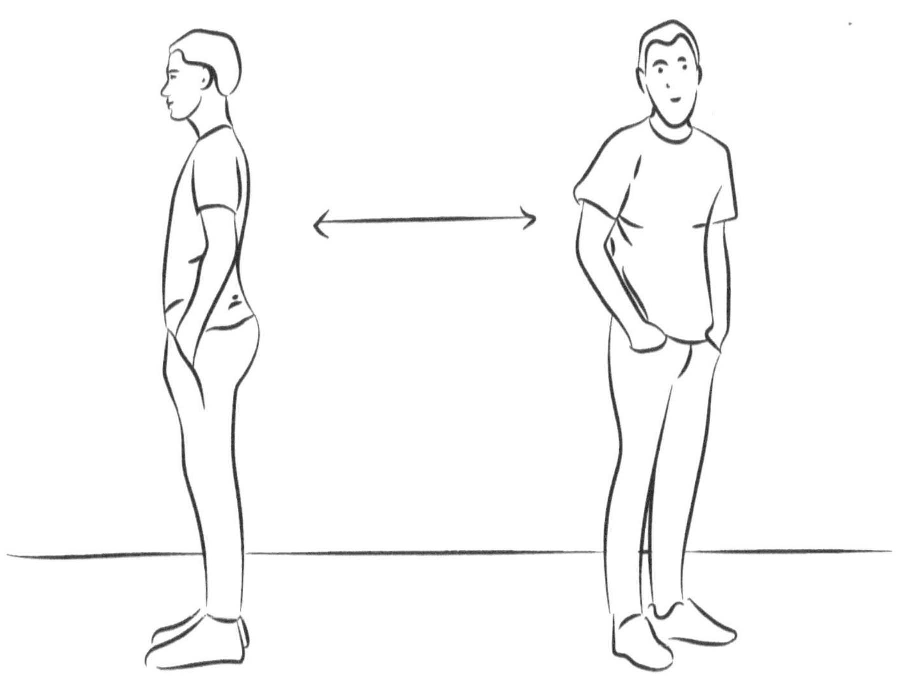

Clients say this to me often.

It usually follows a movement that compresses or expands the spine in a way it hasn't experienced in a long time.

At the end of the last chapter, you explored several exercises—three that were core-focused and three that were general movements with a core emphasis. But what *makes* a core exercise a core exercise? And what makes a stretch for the spine truly a *stretch*?

WHAT DEFINES
A CORE EXERCISE?

For an exercise to be a core exercise, there must be some degree of **compression** through the front of the torso at some point during the exercise.

When you compress, you apply inward pressure. It's like when you squeeze the middle of a full toothpaste tube. The contents shift, just a little bit, and the pressure shifts to either end.

If you squeeze both ends of the toothpaste tube, the pressure shifts again, this time towards the middle of the tube. This means where you compress determines where the pressure goes.

The same is true when you think about applying compression to the front center of the body. One of the easiest ways to do this is change the position of the rib cage or pelvis, tipping one (or both) forward. Any subtle shift in position you make will change the way pressure is being distributed.

The same is true of your breath. Any time you direct the breath to a different area, the pressure in your center shifts.

Before you imagine that I'm suggesting you should walk around with your spine flexed all the time, note the key phrase: *at some point*. Compression is context-dependent—it can be dialed up or down based on the task at hand.

COMPARING TWO MOVEMENTS: GOBLET SQUAT AND CANDLESTICK

Let's look at two exercises from the previous chapter: the **goblet squat** and the **candlestick**.

During the goblet squat, I suggested holding the kettlebell **bottoms up**, meaning the heavy bell points toward the ceiling. This directs the load downward through the hands, which connect to the shoulders.

That positioning encourages the shoulder blades to stabilize in a way that allows the muscles linking the front of the body to the shoulders to create an appropriate level of tension. This naturally places the ribs in a position that, for many people, engages the abdominals—almost like an *upright plank*.

If you think back to the toothpaste analogy, holding the kettlebell in this way is like pressing on the top of the full toothpaste tube. The pressure moves down in the front of the body.

The compression is subtle, but it's more than what you experience when squatting without weight.

BREATH AS PRESSURE REGULATION

The breathing pattern used in the goblet squat was intentional—it helps create **pressure** and **stability** throughout the movement.

- **Inhale:** The diaphragm and pelvic floor move down.

- **Exhale:** The diaphragm and pelvic floor move up.

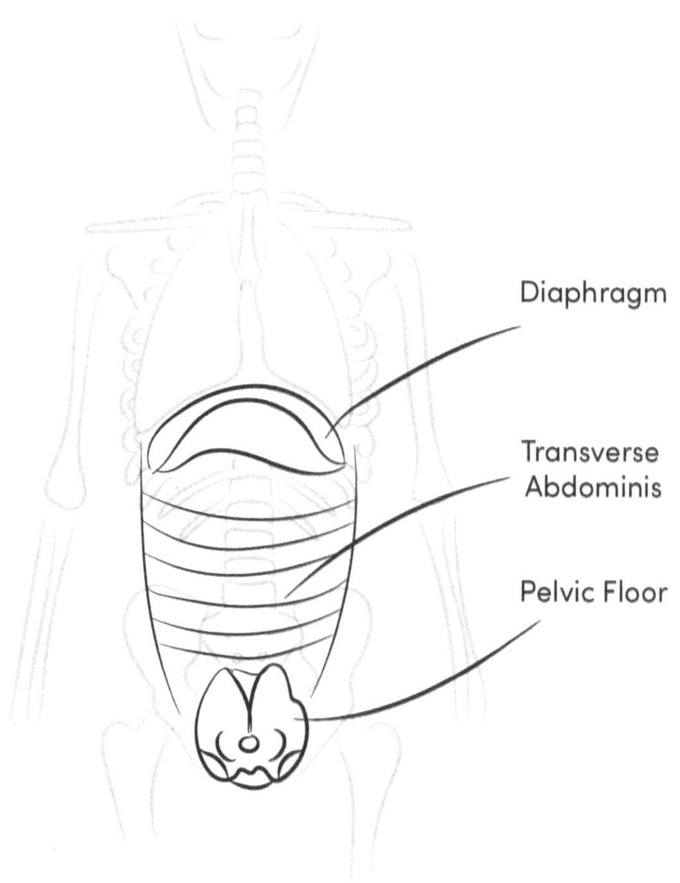

If you recall from Chapter 1, between the diaphragm and pelvic floor lie several deep abdominal muscles (and your viscera). This vertical relationship helps your breath create the *right amount* of tension throughout your torso during movements like a lightly loaded squat.*

THE CANDLESTICK: DIRECT FLEXION

The **candlestick** exercise, on the other hand, creates actual **spinal flexion**.

As your legs reach upward, the flexion point occurs roughly behind the **xiphoid process**—the small cartilaginous tip at the bottom of your sternum.

This area serves as an attachment point for several abdominal muscles, which is why flexing here often produces that familiar sense of deep abdominal work.

WHOLE-BODY COORDINATION

Your torso generates tension based on what your **head, arms, and legs** are doing. You can manipulate any of these to increase or decrease abdominal engagement—or to create a sense of **expansion** and **stretch** instead.

Your musculoskeletal system is like woven fabric—muscles blending seamlessly into one another, forming a continuous network of support throughout your body. You never work a muscle in isolation (even though it may *feel* that way). Every movement is a coordinated effort across multiple regions.

THE POWER OF LEVERS

You know how a small top spins faster than a large one?

The larger top moves more slowly and often wobbles, while the smaller one spins tightly and quickly.

That's because **longer lever arms** (like longer limbs) require more effort to control—they generate more momentum and resist quick change. But they're also excellent for slowing things down or creating power for larger, more dynamic movements.

Creating a short lever requires compression. Creating a long lever requires expansion. If compression is applying inward pressure, you can think of expansion as applying outward pressure so that the volume, or size, increases even though the weight stays the same.

If I squeeze both ends of the toothpaste tube towards each other, the toothpaste gets concentrated towards the center of the tube, taking up less space. If I massage the toothpaste to the ends of the tube, the toothpaste takes up more space, but the amount of the toothpaste stays the same.

Manipulating pressure allows you to manipulate speed. Sometimes it feels good to move fast. Sometimes it feels good to move slow. These basic physical constructs give you the power to alter your experience.

TRY THIS

Come to a **standing position**.

1. Do a few small hops with your **elbows and knees bent**.

    *   Move your elbows as fast as possible.

    *   *Notice:* How fast are you hopping?

2. Pause. Straighten your **arms**.

    *   Begin swinging them back and forth (keep them long).

    *   When it feels natural, use your arms to help you **jump up**.

    *   Find a rhythm—arms swing back as you descend, forward as you rise.

REFLECTION:

» Are your jumps **higher or lower** with long arms compared to bent arms?

» Do you move **faster or slower** with your arms extended?

» How does the change in lever length affect your sense of effort or control?

PHYSICS, PHYSIOLOGY, AND THE ART OF TENSION

Your body is a **biological system**, and the way it moves is governed by the laws of physics. You have the ability to influence both your physiology and how you choose to move.

The best coaches and teachers I've had weren't the ones with the most Tik-Tok followers or the longest list of certifications. They were the ones who understood **physics**—whether or not they used that word—and who knew how to create environments where people felt safe enough to explore and learn. The exceptional ones went a step further: they built in opportunities to play, balancing softness and strength.

You can see this dichotomy of softness and strength in boxing. To deliver a powerful punch—and avoid being knocked backwards—a boxer must be **fully tense** at the moment of impact. But to move quickly and fluidly enough to avoid their opponent, they need a **degree of lightness,** a release of that tension between strikes.

THE SPECTRUM OF TENSION

I've said this before, but it bears repeating:

The amount of **tension** you need at any moment exists on a **spectrum.**

Tension, remember, occurs when something is stretched or strained. Earlier, we talked about compression and expansion; every movement requires an element of compression and expansion. In order for something to compress, something else has to expand. The interplay between compression and expansion creates a degree of tension.

How much tension you're holding right now depends on a variety of factors:

- How well did you sleep last night?

- Did you just get good news? Bad news?

- Are you hungry, full, relaxed, anxious, or depressed?

- What position are you in? Do you feel connected and grounded to a surface? Or are you holding your body upright with your jaw, neck, or shoulders?

MOMENTUM AND MOVEMENT

The physics of movement—your ability to create and control **momentum**—is what allows you to transition fluidly from one moment in time to the next.

If you're doing something artistic, you might pause along the way, shaping, holding, and expressing, before moving again.

How you create that momentum depends on both **internal** and **external input.**

If your internal input (tension) is *more* than necessary, how do you think that affects your movement?

And what if it's *less* than you need? How does that affect your movement?

Finding the right amount of tension for the moment is the art of **spinal intelligence**—the coordination between control and surrender, precision and flow.

TRY THIS: EXPLORING THE SPECTRUM OF TENSION

» Below are two movement patterns, each with two variations—one with more tension, one with less.

» Try both versions. Notice the difference.

When would each variation be most useful?

ROLLING ON THE FLOOR – CREATE TENSION

Setup:

Lie on your back with your arms and legs long.

Movement:

1. Get strong through your arms and legs—reach them away from each other and slightly off the ground (your head will lift).

2. Maintain the reaching sensation as you roll onto your stomach.

   - Don't let your hands or feet touch the floor.

3. Keep the tension as you roll back onto your back.

   - Experiment with your breath; I find it helpful to exhale as I roll, but see what feels best to you.

ROLLING ON THE FLOOR – MINIMAL TENSION

Setup:

Lie on your back with your arms and legs long and relaxed, melting into the floor.

Movement:

1. Gently draw your **right knee** and **right elbow** toward each other.

2. When it feels natural, bring your **left knee** and **left elbow** toward each other—you'll roll onto your right side.

3. Slowly extend your elbows and knees away from each other to roll onto your stomach.

4. Bring your **left elbow and knee** toward each other, followed by the **right elbow and knee,** to roll back onto your side.

EXERCISE 3:
STAGGERED-STANCE SQUAT – CREATE TENSION

Setup:

Begin standing with one foot forward and your back heel lifted.

Movement:

1. Imagine holding an object that weighs **60–70% of your body weight.**

2. Lower the imaginary object toward the floor, maintaining full-body tension.

3. Keep the sense of strength as you stand back up with control.

EXERCISE 4:
STAGGERED-STANCE SQUAT – MINIMAL TENSION

Setup:

Stand with one foot forward and the back heel lifted.

Movement:

1. Allow your torso to remain **relaxed and soft.**

2. Begin reaching the back knee toward the ground, folding your joints gently—like folding a towel.

3. Imagine **helium** lifting you back to standing, unfolding you with ease.

Experiment:

Pretend you're holding the imaginary heavy object only on the way down, or only on the way up.

How does that change the movement?

Where do you have to generate tension?

What matters more than the *amount* of tension you can generate is your ability to create it **at the right time.**

Try the staggered-stance squat again with minimal tension, but this time:

- As you begin the movement, think about the **back of the hip** and **back of the knee** gently pulling toward each other.

- As you prepare to stand up, think about the **front of the hip** and **front of the knee** pulling toward each other.

How does that change the experience?

Do you feel more connected, grounded, or balanced?

All of these exercises are an expression of compression and expansion. There are moments when the movements speed up because the lever arm shortens, and there are moments when the lever arm lengthens, slowing the movement down. I offer suggestions that are designed to shift the pressure, providing different amounts of compression and expansion.

How can you shift the pressure you are experiencing in your body right now? What would you compress? What would you expand?

FINDING FOCUS: **THE MICHAEL PHELPS EXAMPLE**

Compression and expansion don't just happen in the body—they happen in the mind.

When Michael Phelps, the most decorated Olympian of all time, walked out onto the swim deck before a race, he was always wearing headphones—jaw set, eyes focused. Over the years, his playlists included Eminem, Future, Eric Church, and various EDM tracks. He listened until the last possible moment, explaining that music helped him relax and tune into his own world.

Listening to music was Phelps's way of drowning out noise and creating an internal compression, or focus. Moshe Feldenkrais, a physicist and the creator of the somatic movement method that bears his name, called unwanted distraction *parasitic tension*—the unnecessary tension that accumulates when noise pulls your attention away from the task at hand.

You see it in the person whose shoulders are up to their ears while typing. In the cashier whose jaw is clenched as they hand you your receipt. In the athlete who stiffens mid-jump and lands somewhere other than intended.

In a stadium filled with lights, cameras, and shouting fans, the potential for parasitic tension is enormous. Having tools to block it out doesn't just improve focus—it preserves the finely tuned timing of effort and release that makes the difference between a good race and a great one.

NOISE, SHIELDS, AND INSULTS

Phelps understood that in order to focus, eliminate unnecessary tension, and perform his best, he needed a shield.

His shields were noise-canceling headphones and hard-hitting music.

Yours might look different.

Because here's the thing—**when it comes to noise, one person's shield is another person's insult**. If you don't like rap music, listening to rap music isn't going to reduce tension. It's going to create more tension. And if you find the sound of the crowd calming, it no longer becomes noise. It becomes a shield.

Learning to identify your *noise insults*—the sensory inputs that overload or distract you—can dramatically improve how you use your shields, creating the balance essential for spinal intelligence.

COMMON SOURCES OF NOISE

When you think about "noise," you might picture the obvious:

- The neighbor's dog barking.

- The infant crying on a plane.

- The upstairs neighbor's television blaring because they refuse to get hearing aids.

But noise isn't just sound—it's *anything* that disrupts your focus, adds tension, or interferes with awareness.

NOISE, ATTENTION, AND THE SENSORY LANDSCAPE

Today's world is filled with **noise**—so much that we've become habituated to it. We often don't even notice.

The haptic buzz of a smartwatch.

The ping of an incoming message.

The constant hum of the 24-hour news cycle.

Each of these on its own might be a small irritation—a **micro-insult**. But when combined, these small insults accumulate into something larger, tipping the balance of your system and making it harder to recover from the bigger insults that naturally occur throughout life.

Even joyful events—like **childbirth**—are still insults to the system. If you're the one who gave birth, there's the physical insult of the process itself. If you're co-parenting, there's the insult of sleep deprivation and the constant demands of caring for a helpless new being.

These insults shift and evolve over time, balanced by the love and connection of the new relationship.

A MODERN EXAMPLE:
THE NEW PARENT AND THE SMARTWATCH

Imagine you're a new mom on maternity leave. You wear a **smartwatch** to track your steps and monitor your health metrics. You've also enabled text notifications and push notifications from a journalist you follow.

Your baby sleeps a lot, but wakes frequently at night, so you're already tired. During the day, your watch pings about four times an hour with alerts and reminders.

After a few days, you realize you're feeling **drained**.

Those constant notifications are *insults*.

One or two a day would be a small inconvenience—a micro-insult.

But dozens each day become a significant load, especially when layered on top of **sleep deprivation.**

In situations like this, the shields in place aren't enough to counteract all of the insults that are occurring on an hourly basis.

THE SUBJECTIVITY OF NOISE

One of the trickiest things about noise is that it's **personal**.

I mentioned this just a moment ago, but it bears repeating: Michael Phelps's EDM and rap playlist helped him relax and focus. But if you dislike those genres, the same music might make you anxious and tense.

I once gave a talk to a **Navy group** about mindfulness and noise. I used the image of an airplane to illustrate that noise surrounds us all the time—and that what counts as noise depends on perception.

A participant raised his hand and said, "I was a U.S. Navy pilot. I don't fly anymore, but when I hear a plane, I look up. I don't hear noise. I hear peace."

Noise is not the same for everyone.

INTERNAL AND EXTERNAL NOISE

Noise can come from the **outside world** or from **within**.

- **External noise** includes sounds and sensations in your environment—sirens, barking dogs, background television, traffic, or news alerts.

- **Internal noise** might be an ache in your knee, a random intrusive thought, the hum of fatigue, or hunger pangs at an inconvenient time.

Have you ever taken a step and felt an odd zing in your ankle, only for it to disappear on the next step? That's a form of internal noise—a signal that flickers in and out of perception.

Sometimes, noise is actually **information** trying to get your attention. A baby cries because they need something. A persistent ache may be your body's way of saying, *Hey, please pay attention to me.*

When ignored, whispers of discomfort often grow louder—eventually turning into shouts. Learning to **distinguish** between noise that can be tuned out and noise that deserves your attention is one of the central skills of spinal intelligence.

REFLECTION: NOISE OR SIGNAL?

Take a moment to read through the list below.

Next to each item, write when you would consider it noise, and when you would consider it worthy of attention.

☐ Sirens

☐ Dog barking

☐ The sound of the ocean

☐ The sound of rain

☐ The television (if you aren't watching it)

☐ Music you choose

☐ The sound of thunder

☐ A crying baby

☐ Haptic feedback on your phone or smartwatch

☐ A mountain range

☐ The desert landscape

☐ The city

☐ Traffic

☐ The news

☐ Feeling hungry

☐ Feeling anxious

☐ The sensation of physical pain

WHERE DO YOU PLACE YOUR ATTENTION?

Sometimes, the things that require our attention aren't necessarily pleasant—but they affect our lives directly.

How we respond to life's situations depends largely on **where we place our attention**.

It's one of the few things we truly control.

Fortunately, there are many ways to practice this skill.

Before we move on to those techniques, look back at the list. Do any of these sounds or sensations make you feel **calm** just thinking about them?

EXTEROCEPTION AND INTEROCEPTION

Your awareness is shaped by two major sensory systems:

- **Exteroception:** your perception of the external world—sight, sound, smell, touch, and taste.

- **Interoception:** your perception of the internal world—signals like hunger, thirst, heartbeat, and the need to use the bathroom.

Together, these systems create your **moment-to-moment perception** of reality. How you focus your attention can shift whether you're emphasizing an **external** or **internal** aspect of an experience.

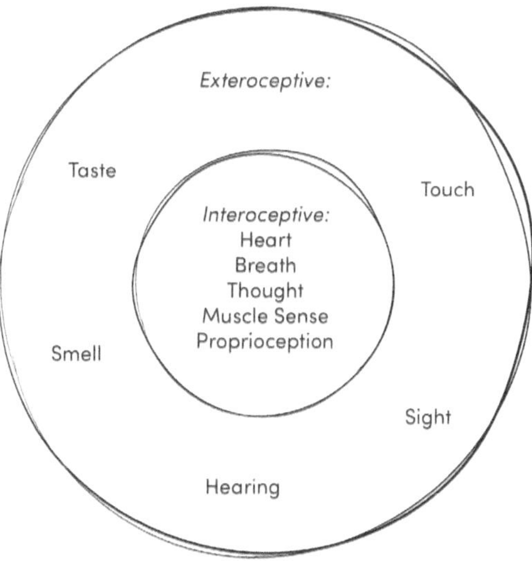

For example:

- When you listen to rain, exteroception processes the sound and rhythm.

- When you feel your chest rise and fall as you breathe in time with it, interoception joins the conversation.

The two systems constantly interact, shaping how you interpret—and move through—the world.

TRY THIS: TWO WAYS TO BREATHE

Step 1:

Focus on your breathing.

Count the duration of your **inhale** and the duration of your **exhale**.

As you count, notice whether your **throat** constricts or relaxes as you breathe.

Step 2:

Now, shift your focus.

As you inhale and exhale, notice the **feeling of air** entering and leaving your nostrils.

Don't try to change anything—just observe.

Can you hear your breath, or is it *silent*?

The first example emphasizes the **interoceptive** aspect of breathing—your awareness of what's happening *inside* your body.

The second emphasizes the **exteroceptive** aspect—your perception of the world *outside* of you.

TAKE A MOMENT TO REFLECT:

Which one do you prefer?

I mentioned earlier you can use your breath to alter the compression and expansion that's occurring internally. It seems fitting that breath can also be a focal point that balances the nervous system. Just like there are many ways to use your breath to alter compression and expansion, you can focus on the internal aspect of the breath or the external aspect of the breath to reduce parasitic tension and internal noise.

DEVELOPING AWARENESS THROUGH BOTH SENSES

Most of us naturally favor one direction of focus—either inward (**interoception**) or outward (**exteroception**). Knowing your preference can be useful. If you tend toward interoceptive awareness, focusing inward might quickly bring a sense of calm or balance. If you prefer exteroception, looking out to the horizon for 60 seconds might be enough to give you a mini-reset.

Developing both creates a more complete and flexible perception of your current moment, just like refining your **body schema** (your internal map of your physical self) provides a fuller understanding of how you move through space.

AWE: WHERE INNER AND OUTER WORLDS MEET

One of the most effective ways to engage both interoceptive and exteroceptive awareness simultaneously is through **nature**.

You know that feeling that washes over you when you look up at a night sky full of stars, stretching endlessly across space?

Or the deep sense of stillness that arises when you reach a mountain summit and gaze out over the vastness below—small, yet fully alive in the moment?

Researchers call this emotion **awe**—a profound sense of wonder or astonishment triggered by something that feels beyond comprehension.

It can arise from a sweeping natural vista or a powerful idea—making it both an **exteroceptive** and **interoceptive** experience.

THE ROLE OF NATURE IN MINDFULNESS

Nature might be the simplest and most accessible source of awe.

It's the sunrise breaking over the horizon. The night sky stretching to infinity. The forest trail humming with stillness. The ocean extending into blue that dissolves into sky.

When you step into nature, your senses open up. You hear layers of sound you don't notice in daily life. Your eyes widen to take in light, depth, and distance. You may even smell subtle shifts in the air or taste salt carried by the wind.

Your exteroceptive and interoceptive senses are always working, but most of the time we tune them out. If we didn't, we'd be overwhelmed by a constant, buzzing stream of sensory data.

When you step away from that everyday buzz and immerse yourself in something larger than yourself, your senses synchronize. This leads to emotions like joy, reverence, or even fear—and, paradoxically, to a diminished sense of self.

That's the irony of awe: when the self gets smaller, connection expands.

The expansiveness of nature reminds you that no matter how much you expand, you are actually quite small. And yet nature can compress an infinite amount of beauty into a tiny space. On a movement retreat in Costa Rica several years ago, I looked down on my way to breakfast one morning and saw what appeared to be a never-ending trail of leaves moving across the path.

They were leaf-cutter ants, each carrying a piece of leaf many times its own body weight toward a destination known only to them. I watched, mesmerized.

Whether you are marveling at insects or staring at the vastness of the ocean, there is a moment where the voice in your head goes quiet and the tension you carry as armor against the noise of daily life simply falls away. It's like a visual massage.

FEAR AND THE EDGE OF AWE

Of course, what one person finds awe-inspiring, another may find terrifying. Standing on a mountain peak may fill one person with peace and give another vertigo.

A little fear, though, can amplify awe.

The vastness of nature can feel like it might swallow you whole—but that very vastness commands focus, quiets internal noise, and brings you wholly into the present moment.

MINDFULNESS AND BALANCE

Nature offers a simple way to integrate the forms of **mindfulness** we discussed in Chapter 4, particularly **focused attention** and **open monitoring**.

Other forms, such as **loving-kindness meditation**, can also restore balance and connection, each with their own unique effects on the nervous system. Practicing mindfulness in any form is ultimately a way to return to **equilibrium**.

For Michael Phelps, **music** was a form of mindfulness—it helped him focus when it mattered most.

For **Simone Biles**, mindfulness meant closing her eyes before competition, taking a moment to turn inward and reconnect before performing.

Both illustrate the same principle:

Intentional awareness is a shield—a way to reduce noise and create space for focused energy.

REFLECTION: MAPPING YOUR SENSORY AWARENESS

I mentioned earlier that developing awareness of both your **internal** and **external** senses can reduce noise and improve focus.

Take a look at the two lists below.

Mark each sense with:

- a √ if it's *easy* for you to focus on

- an × if it's *challenging*

Internal Senses

☐ Heart rate

☐ Breathing

☐ Thoughts

☐ Muscle sense (tension or relaxation)

☐ Proprioception (awareness of where your body is in space)

External Senses

☐ Auditory (hearing)

☐ Visual (seeing)

☐ Taste

☐ Smell

☐ Touch

After you've marked your lists, reflect:

- Do you have more checkmarks on the **internal** or **external** side?

- Or is it fairly balanced?

TEN-MINUTE PRACTICE:
FROM EXTERNAL TO INTERNAL AWARENESS

If you have ten minutes, try this practice.

Before you begin, write down your **mood** and **energy level**.

This example moves from **exteroception** to **interoception**.

If external awareness feels difficult for you, reverse the sequence—start inward, then move outward.

This concept is inspired by **Daniel Siegel's "Wheel of Awareness" practice**, which is described in detail in his book *Aware: The Science and Practice of Presence*.

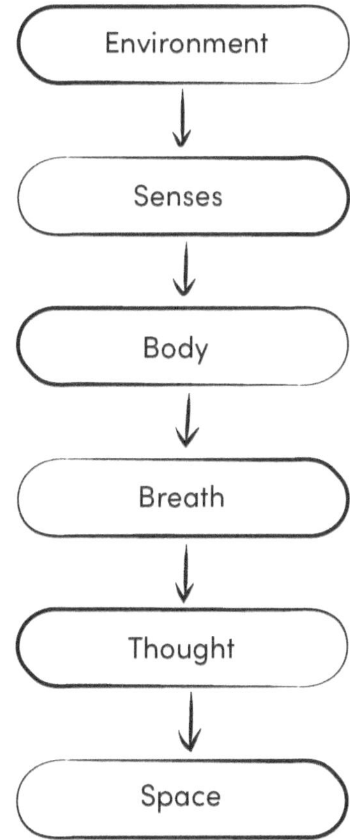

GUIDED PRACTICE: MOVING FROM EXTERNAL TO INTERNAL

Come into a **comfortable position**.

You can be seated, lying down, or standing—whatever allows you to feel supported and at ease.

Take a moment to settle. You'll be here for a while.

STEP 1:
LISTENING (AUDITORY AWARENESS)

Begin by simply listening.

What do you hear?

Observe the sounds around you for several seconds—near and far, soft and sharp.

Notice the layers of sound that make up your environment.

STEP 2:
SEEING (VISUAL AWARENESS)

Now, look around the room.

What do you see?

Let your eyes land on something you find interesting.

Take a few moments to notice its **shape, texture, color**, and **detail**.

STEP 3:
SMELLING (OLFACTORY AWARENESS)

Shift your attention to what you **smell**.

Are there any distinct scents in the room—perhaps the air, fabric, or something faint and familiar?

TOUCH (TACTILE AWARENESS)

Now bring awareness to the **sensation of touch.**

Notice:

- The feeling of your clothes against your skin
- The temperature of the air
- The pressure where your body meets the chair, floor, or ground

Scan slowly, feeling how your skin makes contact with your surroundings.

MOVING INWARD (PROPRIOCEPTIVE AWARENESS)

Begin to sense the **outline of your body.**

Where are your feet? Your legs? Your knees?

Move your awareness upward—into your pelvis, hips, and spine.

Can you sense where they are?

Shift to your **shoulder blades, arms, and hands.**

Can you feel their position in space?

Finally, move your attention to your **neck, throat, head, nose, and eyes.**

Can you sense their position and presence?

BREATH AND HEARTBEAT (INTEROCEPTIVE AWARENESS)

Focus on your **breath.**

Feel the inhale. Feel the exhale.

See if you can sense the pauses—

between inhale and exhale,

between exhale and inhale.

Now, bring your awareness to your **heartbeat.**

If you can't feel it at first, pause and listen.

Can you sense its rhythm—the steady pulse beneath everything else?

RELEASING TENSION (MUSCLE SENSE)

Shift awareness back to your body.

Where do you feel tension?

When you find an area, gently **contract the muscle** a bit more—then **let it go.**

Continue scanning your body.

Each time you encounter tension, **tighten slightly, then release.**

Notice how your body feels as you move through this process.

OBSERVING THOUGHTS (MIND AWARENESS)

Once you've finished your body scan, turn inward toward your **thoughts.**

Watch them as they arise and pass.

Don't try to change or analyze them—just observe.

Each thought is like a cloud drifting through a vast sky.

REFLECTION

When you've completed the practice, pause.

- How do you feel?

- What do you notice about your mood or energy?

- Has your sense of tension shifted?

Write down any reflections, sensations, or insights that stand out.

PRACTICE NOTES

This is a long practice, but any **section** of it can become a **mini-mindfulness exercise**.

All you need is **1-3 minutes** and a **focal point**.

You might focus just on sound, on breath, or on the simple act of feeling your feet on the floor.

WHY IT MATTERS

Using mindfulness to **reduce noise** and improve the flow between the **central executive network, salience network**, and **default mode network** enhances more than focus—it improves your overall **integration**.

This flow strengthens the coordination between **mind and body**, creating a **shield** that enhances your durability—just like physical strength does.

REFLECTION: EVERYDAY NOISE

Before we move on, take a few minutes to write down some of the things you consider noise in your daily life.

Some examples might include:

• The news

• The vibration of your phone

• The sound of the city

• Constant multitasking

• Internal chatter

Which of these could you reduce or reframe to strengthen your shields?

CHAPTER 8: INTEGRATING THE PRACTICES

The following programs are ideas, ways to integrate the concepts from each chapter into a movement practice. You'll find two programs per chapter, each clearly themed.

These are not intended to replace a movement hobby, athletic activity, rehabilitation plan, or strength and conditioning program. Instead, think of them as **supplemental practices** designed to help you tap into your spinal intelligence.

Developing true spinal intelligence—the cultivated awareness of how your spine participates in every movement and the confidence to trust it—requires moving in ways that build body awareness, coordination, strength, and flexibility. These practices are designed to do exactly that.

Movement is easier to understand when you can see it. Next to each practice, you'll find a QR code linking to a companion video of the full sequence, a visual guide to help the exercises feel familiar before you begin.

PRACTICE 1: EMBODIED ANATOMY: SENSING THE SPINE

To *embody*, according to Merriam-Webster, means "to make perceptible." To perceive the spine, it helps to feel how its different parts move and how the surrounding structures support it.

This practice emphasizes **noticing and sensing** your spine.

1. DRAW YOUR SPINE

Begin by drawing a picture of your spine as you imagine it. Don't worry about accuracy—this is simply a way to bring awareness to how you perceive your spine right now.

2. BRIDGE ROLL-DOWNS

1. Lie on your back with your knees bent and your feet on the floor (Photo 1).

2. Lift your hips into a bridge (Photo 2).

3. Roll your spine down slowly, one vertebra at a time, as though each segment is meeting the ground in sequence.

4. Perform 1-2 repetitions, then change your foot position and perform 1-2 more.

5. Change your foot position one more time and repeat 1-2 times.

3. SUPINE ROLLS SIDE TO SIDE (LEGS UP)

1. Lie on your back and lift your feet off the ground.

2. Place your hands on the outside of your thighs (Photo 3).

3. Imagine a line connecting your xiphoid process to your pubic bone.

4. Maintain that line as you roll toward your left shoulder and hip, allowing the right shoulder and hip to lift (Photo 4).

5. Return to center and roll to the opposite side.

6. Repeat 2-4 times in each direction.

4. SIDE PLANK RIB DROPS (NO HIP LIFT)

1. Lie on your right side and prop yourself up on your right forearm, knees bent.

2. Press your right forearm into the floor and lift your right ribs away from the ground (Photo 5).

3. Lower your ribs back down slowly (Photo 6).

4. Repeat 4 times. On the final repetition, maintain the lifted position and breathe naturally for 2–3 breaths.

5. QUADRUPED TO SIT BACK (HANDS OFF FLOOR)

1. Come onto your hands and knees (Photo 7).

2. Rock back toward your heels and notice how your spine and pelvis move.

3. As you rock back, walk your hands toward your knees (Photo 8).

4. Once seated on your heels, slide your hands off the floor and sit upright or stand on your knees, whichever feels more comfortable (Photo 9).

5. Repeat 2–4 times, focusing on creating space through your spine as you move.

REFLECT:

Draw another picture of your spine.

Does it look different from your first drawing? What changed?

PRACTICE 2:
EMBODIED ANATOMY:
SENSING THE TORSO

Begin by writing down **two areas of your torso** where you feel the most supported.

One way to feel more connected to the torso is by sensing the internal actions of the muscles. This practice focuses on noticing how those muscular sensations create stability, movement, and support.

1. SPHINX ROLL-UP

1. Lie on your stomach and prop yourself up on your forearms (Photo 10).

2. Draw your breastbone toward your pubic bone to begin rolling up, keeping your knees on the ground (Photo 11).

3. At the top of the movement, actively pull your breast bone and pubic bone together (Photo 12).

4. Then, move your breastbone away from your pubic bone to roll back down.

5. On the next repetition, initiate the roll-up by moving your pubic bone toward your breastbone.

6. Alternate between initiating from the breastbone and from the pubic bone for 2-4 repetitions, noticing the subtle difference in how your torso responds.

2. PRONE CHEST LIFT

1. Remain on your stomach. Place your hands in a diamond shape on the ground (Photo 13).

2. Reach your head toward your hands, allowing your head and upper chest to gently lift. Optional: straighten your arms as well, like they are sliding the same direction your head is reaching (Photo 14).

3. Lower back down slowly.

4. Repeat 2-4 times, maintaining a smooth, connected movement.

3. ALTERNATIVE PRONE CHEST LIFT

1. Lie on your stomach with your hands again in a diamond shape (Photo 15).

2. Slide your right elbow and right knee toward each other.

3. Reach your head forward, letting it initiate the lift, and allow your gaze to turn slightly over your right shoulder (Photo 16).

4. Lower back down and repeat 2–4 times.

5. Switch sides and repeat the same pattern, noticing any differences between sides.

4. QUADRUPED HAND AND KNEE LIFT

1. Come onto your hands and knees (Photo 17).

2. Lift one hand and one knee at the same time (Photo 18).

3. Try lifting the same-side hand and knee, then the opposite-side hand and knee (Photo 19).

4. Which feels easier? Which feels more stable?

5. Perform 2–4 repetitions on each side, paying attention to how your torso adjusts to maintain balance.

5. SUPINE HARD ROLL (ABDOMINAL EMPHASIS)

1. Lie on your back with your knees bent.

2. Place your right hand behind your head and lift your right foot, keeping the knee bent.

3. Position a yoga block between your right thigh and right elbow. Your head will be off the floor (Photo 20).

4. Press your thigh and elbow gently into the block and begin to roll toward your left.

    - As you roll left, imagine the skin beneath your belly button rotating *right*.

    - As you roll right, imagine it rotating *left* (Photo 21).

5. Perform 2 repetitions, then switch sides.

---

6. Now try the opposite: let the skin beneath your belly button rotate *in the same direction* you roll (right with right, left with left).

   • What changes in how your torso moves and feels?

REFLECT:

Look back at what you wrote at the beginning of the practice.

Do you notice any changes?

Maybe your sense of support shifted, or maybe your awareness of your spine simply feels clearer. Take a moment to notice what feels different.

12

13

14

15

16

17

18

19

20

21

PRACTICE 3: NERVOUS SYSTEM: FEELING CONNECTED

When you begin moving, you automatically influence your nervous system.

Whether you *rev it up* or *downshift* depends on the types of movements you choose and how challenged you feel.

If something feels too difficult, it can create frustration or disconnection—just as not being challenged enough can leave you disengaged. The goal of this practice is to cultivate awareness from your *feet to your head*, helping you feel connected through your whole system.

Before you begin, **rate your current energy level** on a scale from **1–10**.

1. TAPPING

1. Begin standing, with your knees soft and your feet a comfortable distance apart.

2. Use your **left fingertips** to gently tap across your collarbone, down your right arm, and up into your cheeks. Tap anywhere that feels like it needs attention for about **60–90 seconds** (Photo 22).

3. Pause. Notice how you feel.

4. Switch sides and tap with your **right fingertips** for another **60–90 seconds**.

5. Pause again.

6. Finally, tap with **both hands**—along your hip bones, across your back, down your legs, wherever you feel drawn—for another **60–90 seconds** (Photo 23).

7. Pause and take **three slow breaths**, observing how your body feels now.

2. STANDING SINGLE-ARM FIGURE 8S (WITH WEIGHT SHIFT)

1. Stand with your feet wider than shoulder distance.

2. With your **right hand**, trace a large, horizontal figure eight (∞) in front of you, using your entire arm (Photo 24, 25).

---

3. Let your **weight shift** from side to side as your arm moves through the pattern.

4. Complete **4–8 repetitions** with your right arm, then switch sides.

5. When you finish, pause and take a moment to **observe your body**—your breath, your posture, your sense of connection.

3. STANDING ROTATION TO HAND DOWN

(You may want a yoga block or short stool if the floor feels far away.)

1. Stand with your feet wide, toes turned slightly out (Photo 26).

2. Rotate to your **right**, letting the rotation begin from your **feet** so they pivot (Photo 27).

3. As you rotate, place your **left hand** on the floor near your right foot—or on a block if needed (Photo 28).

4. Rotate back to center.

5. Repeat **2–4 times**, then switch sides.

6. Notice how your spine and breath move together as you rotate.

4. HEEL-TO-TOE TO FOOT-OUT-TO-THE-SIDE REACH

1. Begin standing with your feet **staggered**, weight in the **back foot** (Photo 29).

2. Rock your weight forward into your **front foot** as you reach your **back foot** out to the side (Photo 30).

3. Return the back foot to its starting position and rock your weight back onto it.

4. Repeat **2–4 times**, then switch sides.

5. *Something to ponder:* What are your arms doing? Could they help you balance or coordinate the movement?

REFLECT:

After you finish, **reassess your energy level** on a scale from 1-10.

Would you give yourself the same number you did before you started?

28

29

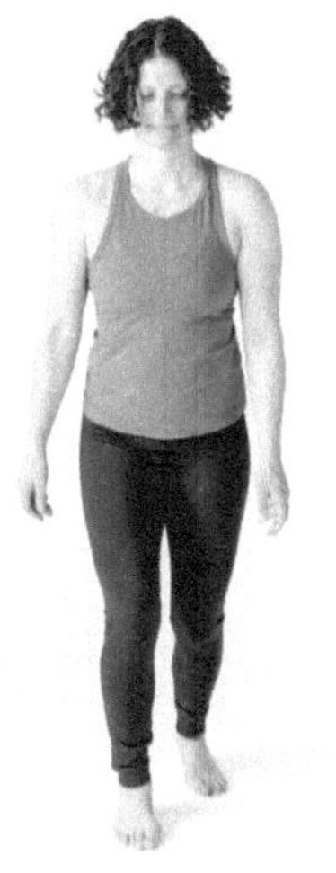

30

PRACTICE 4:
NERVOUS SYSTEM: ENERGY AND FOCUS

There are many ways to shift your state in the present moment.

By integrating the senses—touch, vision, visualization, and breath—you can change how you feel and bring your attention back to the body.

Before you begin, **take a moment to jot down how you currently feel**.

1. SCRUBBING

1. Stand with your feet comfortably apart and your knees soft.

2. Using your hands and fingers, begin **scrubbing your skin**—your jaw, face, and neck; then your chest, arms, and hands; then your belly, low back, hips, and legs (Photo 31).

3. Spend **2–3 minutes** scrubbing.

4. When you finish, pause. **Take three slow breaths** and observe the sensations that remain.

2. SIDE STEP (MINI CURTSY SQUAT TO LATERAL STEP)

Focus on the feet and weight shift.

1. Stand with your feet close together, knees softly bent and responsive.

2. Transfer weight onto your **right foot** as you lightly touch your **left foot** behind the right heel (Photo 32).

3. Step your **left foot** out to the side, shifting your weight onto it (Photo 33).

4. Repeat to the opposite side.

5. Perform **2–4 repetitions** each way, feeling the rhythm of the weight shift.

3. ARMS AROUND A BIG BALL

1. Stand with your feet about shoulder-width apart (or slightly wider).
2. Imagine a large, floating ball in front of you—a *magical ball* suspended in the air (Photo 34).

3. Take your arms all the way around it, tracing the top, bottom, and sides, without touching it (Photo 35).

4. Let your knees bend and your torso fold and unfold as your arms move.

5. Perform **4-6 repetitions**, then pause and sense how you feel.

4. BREATHING (STANDING WITH ARM MOVEMENT)

1. Stand with your feet a comfortable distance apart, knees soft, hands in front of your chest.

2. As you **inhale,** allow the breath to gently move your hands away from each other (Photo 36).

3. As you **exhale,** use the breath to draw your hands *closer together* (Photo 37).

4. Repeat for **3-5 breath cycles**, sensing how your breath moves through your arms and chest.

REFLECT

» After you finish, jot down how you feel now.

» Is it the same as when you began?

31

32

PRACTICE 5:
BASIC STRENGTH

Please note: this is a supplemental program and is not intended to replace an existing strength and conditioning program.

Strength training can feel intimidating—how to do it properly, what equipment to use, and how many sets or reps are needed to "make it work" are common questions.

Fortunately, it doesn't take much to begin. The program below is a **bodyweight series** that requires minimal equipment: just a set of rings, which you can easily find online for about $25.

Each exercise includes **three variations** of the same movement. Choose the version that feels most appropriate for you today.

Before you begin, **take a moment to write down how your body feels.**

____

____

____

1. PUSH-UPS

1. Begin on your hands and knees. Walk your hands forward slightly so there's a gentle angle between your shoulders and knees (Photo 38).

2. Lower your torso toward the floor (Photo 39).

3. Press back up, thinking of your **chest, the skin under your belly button, and your pelvis** moving upward together.

4. Perform **6–12 repetitions.**

Modifications:

- If this feels too challenging, push yourself back into **child's pose** instead of straight up.

- If this feels too easy, perform the movement from a **straight-arm plank position.**

2. TABLE ROWS

1. Position yourself under a sturdy table, railing, or a pair of rings/suspension trainer (Photo 40).

2. Hold on with your hands, knees bent so your body is roughly parallel to the floor.

3. Pull your body upward toward your hands (Photo 41).

4. Lower back down with control.

5. As you pull, imagine initiating the movement from the **armpit all the way down to the pinky finger.**

6. Repeat for **4–8 repetitions.**

3. SQUAT (RINGS OPTIONAL FOR SINGLE-LEG VARIATION)

1. Stand with your feet a comfortable distance apart, holding the rings, holding nothing, or holding a weight (Photo 42).

2. Squat down, imagining your **pinkie toes reaching long** against the floor. (Photo 43)

3. Let your ribs and pelvis move **down and back together** as you lower.

4. Perform **6–10 repetitions.**

To increase the challenge:

- Try lifting one heel, then the other. (Photo 44)

- Try lifting one foot entirely.

- Or play with tempo—descend quickly, then rise slowly, noticing how it feels.

4. STEP OVER, DUCK UNDER

1. Stand with your feet fairly close together (Photo 45).

2. Imagine a **tall fence** on your right side. Step over it with your right leg, letting the **skin of your upper right thigh rotate outward** as you step (Photo 46).

3. Bring your left leg over to join it (Photo 47).

4. Now imagine a **long log** in front of you. Duck under it, keeping your spine smooth and avoiding contact with the "log" (Photo 48, 49).

5. Repeat **3–5 times**, then switch sides.

To progress:

Hold a **weight, medicine ball, or any small weighted object** as you step over and duck under.

Whenever I suggest imagining the skin is rotating, it's just that—a cue to help you sense subtle movement. It's something that can be felt, not seen.

REFLECT

» After you finish, **take a moment to write down how your body feels**.

» Do you notice a difference in strength, awareness, or energy compared to when you started?

Spinal Intelligence

44

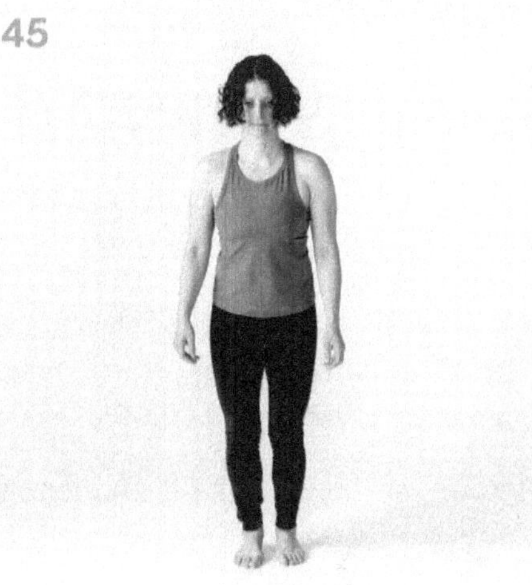

45

46

47

48

49

PRACTICE 6:
BASIC STRENGTH 2

Navigating your own body weight is a valuable skill—and so is navigating an external load.

We lift and carry things all the time: **grocery bags, children, pets, packages.** Life offers constant opportunities to move weight. Practicing in a controlled way helps these daily tasks feel easier and more efficient.

Before you begin, **take a moment to write down how connected to your body you feel.**

For this practice, you'll need a **pair of moderately heavy dumbbells.**

1. QUADRUPED DUMBBELL ROWS

1. Begin on your hands and knees, holding a dumbbell in each hand (Photo 50).

2. Keep your **tailbone free,** and imagine the **skin beneath your belly button** gently moving away from the ground.

3. Press your **left hand** and **both knees** firmly into the floor.

4. With your right arm, **row** the dumbbell by pulling your elbow toward your waist.

   - As you row, imagine the skin beneath your belly button moving slightly to the **left** (Photo 51).

5. Lower the dumbbell down and switch sides.

6. Perform **4–8 repetitions per side.**

2. MAT DUMBBELL PRESSES

1. Lie on your back with your knees bent and a dumbbell in each hand, elbows resting on the floor beside you (Photo 52).

2. Feel your feet connecting with the ground.

3. Press the dumbbells up toward the ceiling (Photo 53).

4. Lower the elbows back down with control.

5. Try inhaling as you press the dumbbells up; then try exhaling as you press.

    • Which version feels more coordinated or natural to you?

6. Repeat **4–8 repetitions.**

3. **SPLIT SQUAT (LOADED)**

1. Stand holding a dumbbell on your **right shoulder** (Photo 54).

2. Step your **left foot back,** lowering your left knee toward the floor as your **left hand touches your right knee** (Photo 55).

3. As you step back, imagine your **right ribs reaching slightly backward.**

4. Return to standing by bringing your left foot forward.

5. Perform **3–6 repetitions,** then switch legs.

4. **GOBLET SQUAT WITH DUMBBELL**

1. Stand with your feet a comfortable distance apart, holding a dumbbell in front of your chest with both hands (Photo 56).

2. Squat down, allowing your **ribs and pelvis to move back and down together** (Photo 57).

3. Stand back up with control.

4. Perform 4-8 repetitions.

REFLECT

>> When you're done, pause for a moment and notice how your body feels.

>> Do you feel more grounded, more connected, or more awake?

FLEXIBILITY

"Mobility is all you need."

While that might not be entirely true, **feeling like you can move easily** plays a major role in wanting to move more. A short morning routine that encourages variety can help you feel more bouncy, awake, and ready for your day.

Before you begin, **write down any areas that feel stiff** or resistant to movement.

____

____

____

These are the same practices included at the end of Chapter 4. As a result, the formatting style differs from the other practices.

PRACTICE 7:
FOCUS ON THE SHOULDERS

RUB AND SENSE

1. Begin standing.

2. Rub around your chest, shoulders, and down your arms.

SHIFT AND DRAW

1. Stand with your feet wide.

2. As you shift your weight side to side, draw a large, horizontal figure eight with your right arm.

3. Let your hand trace the shape. Then try leading with your elbow, then your shoulder.

4. Repeat with the left arm.

SLIDE

1. With feet comfortably apart, slide your shoulders up and down.

2. See if you can focus on the shoulder blades moving up and down (Photo 58, 59).

EYES AND ARMS

1. Make a thumbs-up with your right hand and lift it to eye level.

2. Keep your head still as you move your right arm out to the side, keeping your eyes fixed on your thumb (Photo 60, 61).

3. When you lose sight of it, return to start. Repeat 2–4 times. Then repeat while allowing your head to follow the movement (Photo 62). Repeat both versions with your left hand.

WRAP AND REACH

1. Slide your hands to your elbows.

2. Reach the elbows forward, rounding your spine and head (Photo 63).

3. Lift the elbows up and overhead, as though taking off a sweater (Photo 64).

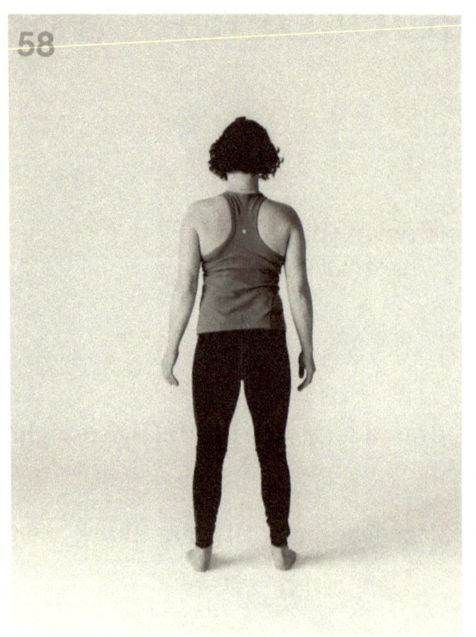

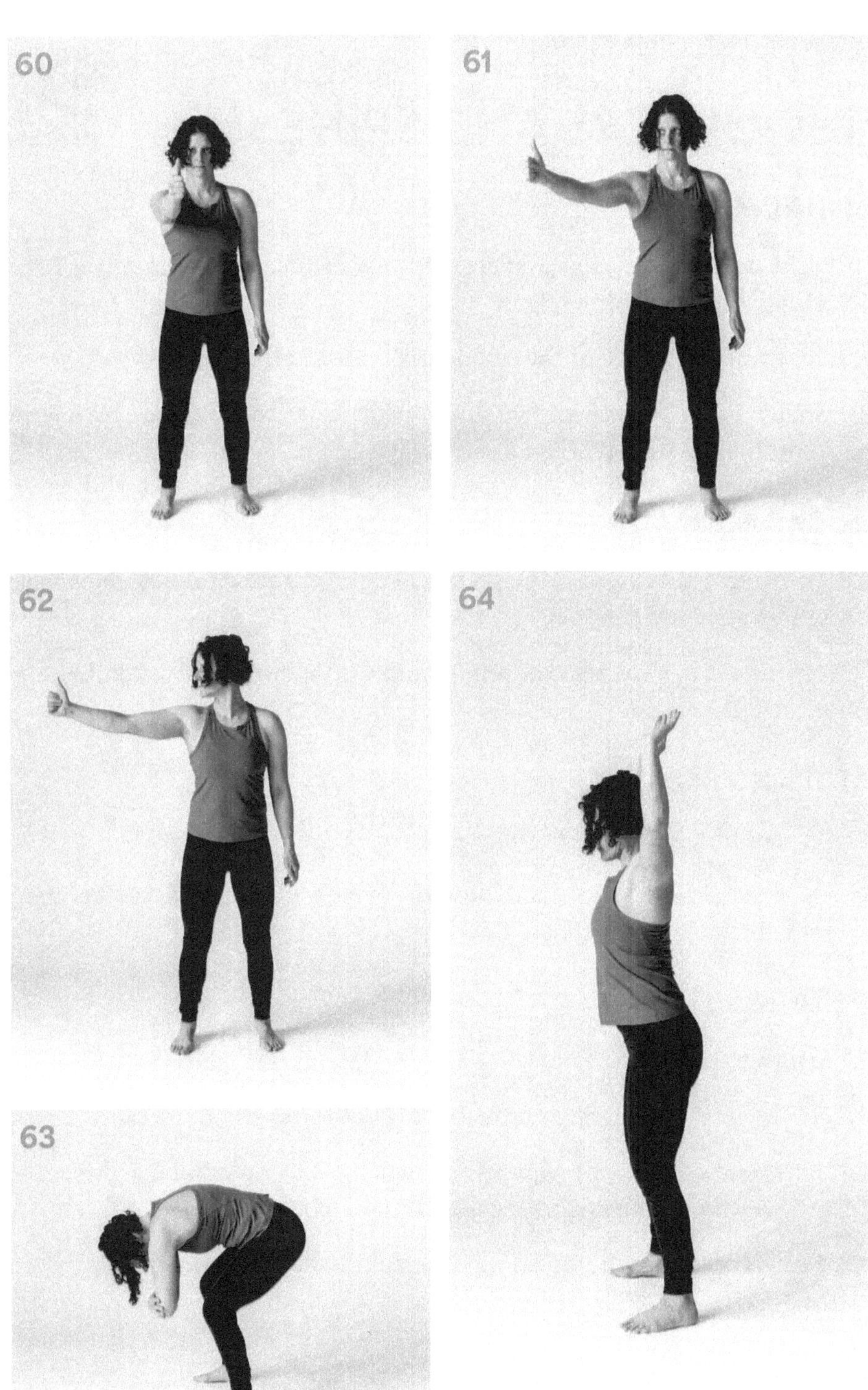

PRACTICE 8:
SHOULDERS AND SPINE

SPINAL MAPPING

1. Begin on your hands and knees. Move your breastbone up toward the ceiling, then toward the floor.

2. Move your belly toward the ceiling, then toward the floor.

3. Finally, bring your shoulders and hips as close together as possible in front, then in back (Photo 65, 66.

ROCK AND REACH

1. Feel your hands against the ground. Rock your hips toward your heels and back several times.

2. As you rock back, reach your right hand a little farther forward, then the left. Do 2-3 rounds.

REST AND BREATHE

1. Sit your hips back toward your heels.

2. Take 2-4 slow breaths, imagining the breath filling the space between your shoulder blades (Photo 67).

ROTATION FLOW

1. Return to hands and knees.

2. Float your knees slightly off the floor (Photo 68).

3. Turn your knees to the right as you pick up your right hand and place it behind you, eyes facing the horizon (Photo 69).

4. Turn back to the left, returning your right hand to the floor.

5. Repeat to the other side.

6. Pause with hands behind you, eyes on the horizon. Let your chest sink, then expand. Do 2-3 times.

SIDE PROP

1. Lie on your right side with knees bent, propped on your right forearm (Photo 70).

2. Let your right ribs drop toward the floor, then lift away a few times. You have the option of lifting the right hip off the floor when you lift the right ribs away from the floor.

3. Keeping the ribs lifted and with the option of having the right hip lifted, reach your left hand toward the ceiling and make small arm circles (Photo 71).

4. Repeat on the other side.

PRACTICE 9: SPINE

BOUNCE AND FEEL

1. Stand tall and lightly bounce up and down for about 30 seconds, noticing the vibration through your body.

DIVE AND ROLL

1. Imagine an invisible wall in front of you. Dive under it, then extend up on the other side (Photo 72, 73, 74).
2. Repeat 3-4 times.
3. Then reverse—extend down and roll back up.

CIRCLE THE SPACE

1. Stand with your feet wide as if holding a large beach ball (Photo 75).
2. Move the "ball" in a big circle, touching the floor, walls, and ceiling (Photo 76, 77).
3. Perform 4-5 circles in one direction, then switch. Does one direction feel easier?

WALL ROTATION

1. Place your hands on a wall, fingers pointing away from each other (Photo 78).
2. Step your right foot behind your left as you rotate your body away from the wall (your right hand will lift) (Photo 79, 80).
3. Return to start, rotating back toward the wall—foot, hips, chest. Which sequence feels more natural—rotating away from the wall or back towards the wall?
4. Repeat on the other side.

BREATHING AROUND THE BALL

1. Imagine your arms are wrapped around a large beach ball.
2. As you inhale, open your arms away from the ball (Photo 81).
3. As you exhale, return to wrap around it (Photo 82).
4. Repeat 3–5 times.

72
73
74
75
76
77

PRACTICE 10:
SPINE AND HIPS

ROUND AND EXTEND

1. On hands and knees, round your back as you reach your hips back.

2. Extend your back as you shift your hips forward.

3. Repeat 2-4 times.

SLIDE AND FEEL

1. Stay on your hands and knees and take your knees slightly wider.

2. Slide your feet to the right as you sit your hips back.

3. Return to center as you come forward. Notice how your back responds as you move.

4. After 4-6 rounds, slide and reach your hips back until you find yourself in a seated 90/90 position.

5. Repeat to the other side.

ROLL AND RISE

1. Come into a 90/90 position with your right knee in front and extend your left leg (Photo 83).

2. Place your right hand on the floor slightly behind your right hip (fingers can point away).

3. Turn your palm up toward the ceiling and bring your cheek toward your palm, rolling onto your side, then your back (Photo 84, 85).

4. Return by bringing your cheek to your palm and pressing yourself back up.

5. Do 2-4 times, then switch sides.

What does your spine do to lower you? What helps you come back up? How can your extended leg make it easier?

83

84

85

PRACTICE 11:
HIPS AND FEET

KNEE CIRCLES

1. Stand with your hands on your knees (Photo 86).

2. Circle the knees 3-4 times in each direction (Photo 87).

WALK THE HANDS

1. Slide your hands down your shins to the floor and walk them forward a few steps. Let your knees reach toward the floor—they may even touch.

2. Walk your hands back to lift the knees and return upright.

3. Repeat 2-4 times.

SHIFT AND LIFT

1. From hands and knees, walk your hands around your knees, shifting weight back until your knees lift slightly off the ground (Photo 88).

2. Lower and repeat 2-4 times.

SLIDE AND REACH

1. From hands and knees, keep the skin of your left foot in contact with the floor as you slide it straight back (Photo 89).

2. Once extended, reach it out to the left, maintaining floor contact (Photo 90).

3. Do 2-4 times.

4. On the final repetition, slide the foot out, shift your hips back, and lift your chest and hands (Photo 91).

5. Slide your hands back down to the floor and return to start.

6. Repeat 2-4 times on each side.

SEATED WEIGHT SHIFT

1. Sit with your right foot on the floor (knee pointing up) and your left foot tucked behind the right knee (Photo 92). (Sit on support if needed.)

2. Reach your right knee forward, using your hands on the floor to help you weight-shift. Feel the weight travel into the ball of your right foot (Photo 93).

3. Return to start and repeat 2–4 times, then switch sides.

4. ***Option:*** *After reaching the knee forward several times, reach it forward and slightly left so it aligns with your left knee.*

5. Sit back on your heels or remain upright, then reverse the movement to return.

REFLECT:

» After you finish each practice, take a moment to notice—has your sense of stiffness changed?

PRACTICE 12: FOCUSED ATTENTION

There are an infinite number of ways to direct your attention while you move.

You might focus on something **internal**—a body part, a sensation, or the breath—or something **external**, like a point in space or an imagined object. You can use **visualization**, or you can explore through **play-based tasks**.

Before you begin, **take a moment to reflect on your current awareness of your spine.**

Can you envision what it looks like? Can you sense its shape or how it moves?

QUADRUPED: **TAIL-BASED MOVEMENTS**

1. Begin on your hands and knees.

2. Imagine you have a **tail**. Move it up toward the ceiling and down toward the floor.

3. Wag your tail side to side.

4. For the next **90 seconds**, continue exploring—can you move from your tail in a way that influences the rest of you?

Notice how movement initiated from the tail ripples through your spine, pelvis, and shoulders.

STANDING: **PUBIC BONE-BASED MOVEMENT (INCLUDING ROTATION)**

1. Stand with your feet slightly wider than hip distance.

2. Shift your **pubic bone** to the right—notice how your left leg may get lighter.

3. Shift your pubic bone to the left.

4. Rotate your pubic bone to the right. Adjust your feet as needed.

5. Rotate it to the left.

6. Spend about **90 seconds** initiating movement from your pubic bone—shifting, circling, or rotating.

Where does the movement travel? What feels stable? What feels free?

HANDS AND KNEES: BACK OF RIB CAGE MOVEMENT

1. Come onto your hands and knees.

2. Move your **rib cage** up toward the ceiling, then down toward the floor.

3. Move the rib cage **back toward your heels, then forward away from them.**

4. Rotate the rib cage to the right, then to the left.

5. For the next **90 seconds**, explore moving from the back of your rib cage.

Your hands don't need to stay on the floor—but return to them periodically to reset your sense of support.

STANDING: XIPHOID PROCESS MOVEMENT

1. Stand comfortably.

2. Allow your **xiphoid process** (the small bone at the base of your breastbone) to move back, then forward.

3. Allow it to rotate right, then left.

4. Let it move up, then down.

5. Spend **90 seconds** exploring gentle movement initiated from this point.

How does it affect your breath, posture, or balance?

CRAWLING:

1. Begin on your hands and knees.

2. Crawl forward—either with your knees on the floor or hovering slightly above it.

3. As you crawl, keep your spine **still** for a few steps.

4. Then, allow your spine to **move freely**, rippling as you crawl.

5. Continue for **60–90 seconds**, alternating between stillness and motion.

Which version feels more natural or enjoyable to you?

PRACTICE 13: WHAT HAPPENS IF?

One way to build curiosity and adaptability in your movement is to take something familiar and ask,

"What happens if…?"

What happens if I lead with my elbow?

What happens if I look first?

What happens if I let myself fall—or resist the movement?

Exploring these small variations can change the entire experience.

Before you begin, **scan your body from head to toe.**

Notice if you feel any areas of tension or holding.

SPLIT STANCE LOWERING (TWO VARIATIONS):

1. Begin in a **split stance** position with one foot forward and the back heel slightly lifted (Photo 94).

2. Gently lower your **back knee** toward the ground. Try this **2–3 times** (Photo 95).

3. Then, pull your **front hip** toward your front heel. Try this 2–3 times.

4. Switch sides and repeat.

Notice what changes when you shift the focus of initiation—from the back knee to the front hip.

THROWING A FRISBEE (TWO VARIATIONS):

1. Stand with your feet a comfortable distance apart (Photo 96).

2. Imagine throwing a frisbee with your right hand, moving as you naturally would (Photo 97).

3. After a few throws, try **leading with your elbow** as you throw.

4. Then, try **leading with your wrist**.

5. After experimenting, switch sides and repeat.

Which version feels smoother? Which challenges your coordination?

ROLLING UP (TWO VARIATIONS):

1. Lie on your back with your knees bent and feet flat—or legs long, if preferred.

2. Reach your hands towards the ceiling.

3. Reach your hands toward your knees and your head toward your knees, **rolling up** as far as you can (Photo 98).

4. Roll back down. Repeat **2-3 times**.

5. On your next round, **place your left hand on your left thigh** while reaching your right hand across toward your left knee (Photo 99, 100). Roll up as far as you can, then roll back down.

6. Repeat **2-3 times** and switch sides.

Which version feels easier? Which feels more coordinated or fluid?

REFLECT:

After you finish, take a moment to notice how your body feels.

» Did exploring "what happens if" change your sense of coordination or focus?

» Often, it's not about doing more—it's about paying attention to what happens when you do something *just a little differently.*

94

95

96

97

98

99

100

PRACTICE 14:
INTEGRATION

Integration is a craft. It requires curiosity, trial and error, and a willingness to explore what works—and what doesn't.

To give you a sense of how to integrate the concepts in this book, I've put together two longer practices. You'll recognize some exercises from previous chapters and discover a few new variations. They're arranged to support **body awareness, flexibility, strength, and the mind–body connection,** but they're not the only way.

You can apply these same concepts to any movement practice you enjoy. And if you don't currently have one, this is a good place to start.

WARM-UP:

CAT-COW VARIATION:

1. Begin on your hands and knees with both your hands and knees slightly staggered (Photo 101).

2. Round and arch your spine a few times (Photo 102, 103).

3. Change the stagger of your hands and knees, then continue rounding and arching.

4. Spend about **30–45 seconds**, periodically shifting your hand and knee placement as you move.

TAKE OFF A SWEATER:

1. Come into a **wide-legged squat** with your head hanging down.

2. Hold your elbows with your hands.

3. Reach your elbows forward as you round your spine and begin to lift your torso upright.

4. Keep reaching until your elbows come all the way overhead, as though removing a sweater.

5. Let go and open your arms wide.

6. Repeat **4–6 times.**

Perform the following movements one after the other for **2–4 sets,** resting as needed.

GOBLET SQUAT:

1. Stand with your feet comfortably apart, holding a dumbbell at your chest.

2. Squat down, letting your **ribs and pelvis move back and down together.**

3. Stand back up with control.

4. Repeat **4–8 times.**

SPHINX ROLL-UP:

1. Lie on your stomach and prop yourself up on your forearms.

2. Draw your breastbone toward your pubic bone to begin rolling up. Keep your knees on the ground.

3. Move your breastbone away from your pubic bone to roll back down.

4. On the next repetition, initiate the roll-up by moving the **pubic bone toward the breastbone.**

5. Alternate between initiating from the breastbone and the pubic bone for **2–4 rounds.**

STEP TO ROW:

1. Stand holding a dumbbell in your **left hand** (Photo 104).

2. Step your **left foot forward**. Place your right hand on your left thigh (Photo 105).

3. Row the dumbbell back with your left arm (Photo 106).

4. Step your left foot back to the starting position.

5. Repeat **6–8 times,** then switch sides.

TRIPOD GET-UP:

1. Begin in a **half-kneeling** position with your right foot forward and slightly to the right (Photo 107).

2. Place your **left hand** on the floor as you pivot your **left knee out** and **left heel in** (Photo 108).

3. Press through your right foot and left hand to **stand all the way up** (Photo 109).

4. Reverse the movement to lower back down, pivoting your **left knee in** and **heel out** as your hand returns to the floor.

5. Repeat **4–6 times**, then switch sides.

QUADRUPED ROCKING:

1. Come onto your hands and knees.

2. Rock your hips back toward your heels, then forward again.

3. As you rock, experiment with your spine:

   - Let it round.

   - Let it arch.

   - Let your tail move freely—up toward the ceiling, then between your legs.

4. Spend **45–60 seconds** exploring.

BREATHING:

1. Lie on your back with your knees bent and feet flat on the ground.

2. Rest your arms wherever comfortable.

3. As you inhale, imagine inflating a **balloon beneath your collarbones, expanding toward your armpits.**

4. As you exhale, feel the balloon gently deflate.

5. Repeat for **4–6 breaths.**

   - Inhale through your nose.

   - Exhale softly out your mouth, as if sighing or making a gentle "shhh" sound.

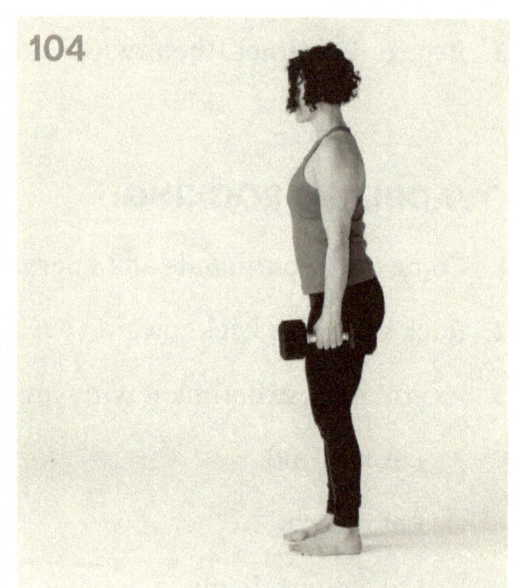

PRACTICE 15:
INTEGRATION

This second integration practice layers strength, coordination, and awareness—blending concepts you've already explored into a flowing, full-body sequence.

CRAWLING:

1. Begin on your hands and knees.

2. Crawl forward a few steps (Photo 110).

3. Crawl backward a few steps.

4. Crawl to the right, then to the left.

5. Crawl in a circle clockwise, then counterclockwise.

6. Spend **90–120 seconds** exploring different directions and rhythms.

Once you're comfortable, try crawling with your knees slightly lifted off the ground.

FIGURE 8:

1. Stand with your feet wider than shoulder distance.

2. With your **left arm**, trace a large horizontal figure eight (∞).

3. Let your weight shift naturally as your arm moves.

4. Perform **4–6 repetitions**, then switch sides.

CHIN-UP OR SHOULDER SHRUGS:

1. Hold onto a bar with your palms facing away from you (Photo 111).

2. Keep your arms straight and pull the bar down slightly, **shrugging your shoulders**.

3. Allow your shoulders to release back up.

4. Repeat **8–10 times.**

5. If this feels easy, turn your palms to face you and pull your **chin over the bar,** using your feet for assistance as needed (Photo 112).

6. Lower down slowly.

7. Repeat **2–6 repetitions.**

PLANK YOGA BLOCK WALK:

1. Begin in a straight-arm plank with your hands on yoga blocks.

If plank feels uncomfortable, come to hands and knees—either with your knees down or hovering slightly above the ground (Photo 113).

2. Follow this sequence, pairing breath and movement:

   - **Inhale:** Press your right hand into the block and lift your left hand (Photo 114).

   - **Exhale:** Place your left hand on the ground inside the block.

   - **Inhale:** Press your left hand into the ground and lift your right hand.

   - **Exhale:** Place your right hand on the ground inside the block (Photo 115).

   - **Inhale:** Press your right hand into the ground and lift your left hand.

   - **Exhale:** Return the left hand to the block.

   - **Inhale:** Press your left hand into the block and lift your right hand.

   - **Exhale:** Return the right hand to the block.

3. Repeat for **2–6 full cycles.**

If coordinating with the breath feels too complex, simply focus on the hand pattern and make sure you're breathing naturally.

SPLIT SQUAT:

1. Stand holding a dumbbell on your **right shoulder** (Photo 116).

2. Step your **left foot back,** lowering your left knee toward the floor as your **left hand touches your right knee** (Photo 117).

3. As you step back, imagine your **right ribs reaching backward**.

4. Return to standing by stepping the left foot forward.

5. Repeat **3–6 times**, then switch legs.

SQUAT TO SIDE ROLL:

1. Begin in a squat (heels can stay down or lift slightly) (Photo 118).

2. Place your hands on the floor, coming to a **hands and knees** position (Photo 119).

3. Lower your **right shoulder and right hip** to the floor, rolling onto your back (Photo 120).

4. Continue rolling until you come back to hands and knees.

5. Shift your weight back into a squat, lift your hands, and stand.

6. Repeat **4–8 times**, alternating directions each round.

COOL-DOWN:

SUPINE TORSO ROCKING:

1. Lie on your back and **hug your knees in** toward your chest.

2. Gently rock side to side.

3. Keep your breathing easy.

4. Spend **30–45 seconds** gently rocking.

BREATHING:

1. Lie on your back with your knees bent and feet flat.

2. Rest your arms comfortably at your sides.

3. Inhale through your nose, imagining your breath riding an elevator **down the back of your throat, through your torso, and into your pelvis.**

4. Exhale softly out your mouth, feeling the breath ride the elevator **back up** through your torso and out into the world.

5. Repeat for **6–8 breaths,** noticing how your body settles and expands with each cycle.

CLOSING THOUGHTS

I began this book by discussing the **physical aspects** of spinal intelligence.

But to truly embrace it, spinal intelligence must include more than the physical—it requires awareness, attention, and a willingness to open yourself to the world around you.

When you choose to **build your shields**, you make it easier to navigate life's insults and maintain balance, even when the world is trying to knock you off your feet.

Through durability, your **movement** changes.

Your **interactions** change.

Your **perception** of the world changes.

This is the heart of spinal intelligence: an embodied awareness that lets you move through life with steadiness, curiosity, and connection. It's the cultivated awareness of the very center of you—the sense of it, how it responds when you move, and the confidence that it will support you.

Both the concepts and the exercises you learned are a starting place. It's kind of like learning to cook—once you learn how things work, it becomes easier to improvise and create the dish with the flavors you truly want. But before you improvise, spend a little time repeating some of the exercises and getting to know how you respond and what they feel like.

If you want to maximize your results, cultivate the shields in other areas of your life. Embrace the power of sleep, and take time periodically to check in with your shields—you might be surprised how much shifts when you do.

Thank you so much for joining me on this journey. I can't wait to hear where it takes you.

Warmly,
Jenn

CHAPTER NOTES

CHAPTER ONE

Ambattu, L. A., & Yeo, L. Y. (2023). Sonomechanobiology: Vibrational stimulation of cells and its therapeutic implications. *Biophysical Reviews*, 4(2), Article 021301. https://doi.org/10.1063/5.0127122

Anderson, B. W., Holme, M. R., Alkhammash, L., & Burns, B. (2023). Anatomy, thorax, xiphoid process. In *StatPearls*. StatPearls Publishing. https://www.ncbi.nlm.nih.gov/books/NBK526082/

Britannica Editors. (2025, October 27). Force. *Encyclopedia Britannica.* https://www.britannica.com/science/force-physics

Flynn, W., & Vickerton, P. (2023, July 24). Anatomy, abdomen and pelvis: Abdominal wall. In *StatPearls*. StatPearls Publishing. https://www.ncbi.nlm.nih.gov/books/NBK551649/

Izzo, R., Guarnieri, G., Guglielmi, G., & Muto, M. (2013). Biomechanics of the spine. Part I: Spinal stability. *European Journal of Radiology*, 82(1), 118–126. https://doi.org/10.1016/j.ejrad.2012.07.024

Mitchell, B., Imonugo, O., & Tripp, J. E. (2025). Anatomy, back, extrinsic muscles. In *StatPearls*. StatPearls Publishing. https://www.ncbi.nlm.nih.gov/books/NBK537216/

Merriam-Webster. (n.d.-a). *Intelligence.* In *Merriam-Webster.com* dictionary. Retrieved March 26, 2026 from https://www.merriam-webster.com/dictionary/intelligence

Rahman, S., & Das, J. M. (2023). Anatomy, head and neck: Cervical spine. In *StatPearls*. StatPearls Publishing. https://www.ncbi.nlm.nih.gov/books/NBK557516/

Sassack, B., & Carrier, J. D. (2023). Anatomy, back, lumbar spine. In *StatPearls*. StatPearls Publishing. https://www.ncbi.nlm.nih.gov/books/NBK557616/

Stretanski, M. F., Hu, Y., & Mesfin, F. B. (2025). Disk herniation. In *StatPearls*. StatPearls Publishing. https://www.ncbi.nlm.nih.gov/books/NBK441822/

Waxenbaum, J. A., Reddy, V., & Futterman, B. (2023). Anatomy, back, intervertebral discs. In *StatPearls*. StatPearls Publishing. https://www.ncbi.nlm.nih.gov/books/NBK470583/

Waxenbaum, J. A., Reddy, V., & Futterman, B. (2023). Anatomy, back, thoracic vertebrae. In *StatPearls*. StatPearls Publishing. https://www.ncbi.nlm.nih.gov/books/NBK459153/

CHAPTER TWO

Biadgo, G. H., Tsegay, G. S., Mohammednur, S. A., & Gebremeskel, B. F. (2021). Burden of neck pain and associated factors among sewing machine operators of garment factories in Mekelle City, Northern Part of Ethiopia, 2018: A cross-sectional study. *Safety and Health at Work*, 12(1), 51–56. https://doi.org/10.1016/j.shaw.2020.10.002

Costa, M. V. dos S., Raulino, L. T. da S., da Silva Júnior, R. R., & Fernandes, T. A. A. de M. (2024). Association of text neck with the appearance of neck pain: Systematic review. *Coluna/Columna*, 23(3), Article 285741. https://doi.org/10.1590/S1808-185120242303285741

de Zoete, R. M. J. (2023). Exercise therapy for chronic neck pain: Tailoring person-centred approaches within contemporary management. *Journal of Clinical Medicine*, 12(22), 7108. https://doi.org/10.3390/jcm12227108

Kawtharani, A. A., Chemeisani, A., Salman, F., Haj Younes, A., & Msheik, A. (2023). Neck and musculoskeletal pain among dentists: A review of the literature. *Cureus*, 15(1), e33609. https://doi.org/10.7759/cureus.33609

Rani, B., Paul, A., Chauhan, A., Pradhan, P., & Dhillon, M. S. (2023). Is neck pain related to sagittal head and neck posture? A systematic review and meta-analysis. *Indian Journal of Orthopaedics*, 57(3), 371–403. https://doi.org/10.1007/s43465-023-00820-x

Resende, P. A., Correia, I. M. T., Ferreira, A. de S., Meziat-Filho, N., & Lunkes, L. C. (2025). Neck pain and text neck using Hill's criteria of causation: A scoping review. *Journal of Bodywork and Movement Therapies*, 42, 132–138. https://doi.org/10.1016/j.jbmt.2024.10.023

Salve, U. R. (2015). Prevalence of musculoskeletal discomfort among workers engaged in jewelry manufacturing. *Indian Journal of Occupational and Environmental Medicine*, 19(1), 44–55. https://doi.org/10.4103/0019-5278.157008

West, C. H. (2024, September 18). What eye conditions does Olympic medalist Stephen Nedoroscik have? *Brain & Life*. https://www.brainandlife.org/articles/what-conditions-does-olympic-medalist-stephen-nedoroscik-have

CHAPTER THREE

Barbari, V., Carbone, M. M., Storari, L., Testa, M., & Maselli, F. (2024). The effectiveness and optimal dose of resistance training in patients with subacute and persistent low back-related leg pain: A systematic review. *Cureus*, 16(3), e57278. https://doi.org/10.7759/cureus.57278

Basketball Reference. (n.d.). LeBron James stats, height, weight, position, draft status and more. Sports Reference. Retrieved September 18, 2025, from https://www.basketball-reference.com/players/j/jamesle01.html

Bengtsson, V., Aasa, U., Öhberg, F., & Berglund, L. (2022). Thoracolumbar and lumbopelvic spinal alignment during the deadlift exercise: A comparison between men and women. *International Journal of Sports Physical Therapy*, 17(6), 1063-1074. https://doi.org/10.26603/001c.37859

ESPN. (n.d.). LeBron James career stats - NBA. ESPN. Retrieved September 28, 2025, from https://www.espn.com/nba/player/stats/_/id/1966/lebron-james

Haider, S. (2026, February 2). LeBron James receives 'worst 2025-26 performer' rating before NBA all-star game. Athlon Sports. https://sports.yahoo.com/articles/lebron-james-receives-worst-2025-172537296.html

Burtscher, J., Strasser, B., D'Antona, G., Millet, G. P., & Burtscher, M. (2023). How much resistance exercise is beneficial for healthy aging and longevity? *Journal of Sport and Health Science*, 12(3), 284-286. https://doi.org/10.1016/j.jshs.2022.11.004

Girotti, M., Adler, S. M., Bulin, S. E., Fucich, E. A., Paredes, D., & Morilak, D. A. (2018). Prefrontal cortex executive processes affected by stress in health and disease. *Progress in neuro-Psychopharmacology & Biological Psychiatry*, 85, 161-179. https://doi.org/10.1016/j.pnpbp.2017.07.004

Herring, M. P., & Meyer, J. D. (2024). Resistance exercise for anxiety and depression: Efficacy and plausible mechanisms. *Trends in Molecular Medicine*, 30(3), 204-206. https://doi.org/10.1016/j.molmed.2023.11.016

Marinelli, R., Parker, A. G., Levinger, I., Bourke, M., Patten, R., & Woessner, M. N. (2024). Resistance training and combined resistance and aerobic training as a treatment of depression and anxiety symptoms in young people: A systematic review and meta-analysis. *Early Intervention in Psychiatry*, 18(8), 585–598. https://doi.org/10.1111/eip.13528

Merriam-Webster. (n.d.-b). Strength. In Merriam-Webster.com dictionary. Retrieved March 2026, from https://www.merriam-webster.com/dictionary/strength

Mueller, J., Weinig, J., Niederer, D., Tenberg, S., & Mueller, S. (2023). Resistance, motor control, and mindfulness-based exercises are effective for treating chronic nonspecific neck pain: A systematic review with meta-analysis and dose-response meta-regression. *Journal of Orthopaedic & Sports Physical Therapy*, 53(8), 420–459. https://doi.org/10.2519/jospt.2023.11820

Saraceni, N., Kent, P., Ng, L., Campbell, A., Straker, L., & O'Sullivan, P. (2020). To flex or not to flex? Is there a relationship between lumbar spine flexion during lifting and low back pain? A systematic review with meta-analysis. *Journal of Orthopaedic & Sports Physical Therapy*, 50(3), 121–130. https://doi.org/10.2519/jospt.2020.9218

Santos, P. D. G., Vaz, J. R., Correia, J., Neto, T., & Pezarat-Correia, P. (2023). Long-term neurophysiological adaptations to strength training: A systematic review with cross-sectional studies. *Journal of Strength and Conditioning Research*, 37(10), 2091–2105. https://doi.org/10.1519/JSC.0000000000004543

Syroyid, I., Cavero-Redondo, I., & Syroyid, B. (2022). Effects of resistance training on pain control and physical function in older adults with low back pain: A systematic review with meta-analysis. *Journal of Geriatric Physical Therapy*, 46(3), E113–E126. https://doi.org/10.1519/JPT.0000000000000374

Yip, D. W., Awosika, A. O., & Lui, F. (2024). Physiology, motor cortical. In *StatPearls*. StatPearls Publishing. https://www.ncbi.nlm.nih.gov/books/NBK542188/

Zemková, E. (2022). Strength and power-related measures in assessing core muscle performance in sport and rehabilitation. *Frontiers in Physiology*, 13, 861582. https://doi.org/10.3389/fphys.2022.861582

CHAPTER FOUR

Alizadeh, S., Daneshjoo, A., Zahiri, A., Anvar, S. H., Goudini, R., Hicks, J. P., Konrad, A., & Behm, D. G. (2023). Resistance training induces improvements in range of motion: A systematic review and meta-analysis. *Sports Medicine*, 53(3), 707–722. https://doi.org/10.1007/s40279-022-01804-x

Biles, S. (n.d.). Overcoming fear [Video]. In Simone Biles teaches gymnastics fundamentals. MasterClass. https://www.masterclass.com/classes/simone-biles-teaches-gymnastics-fundamentals/chapters/overcoming-fear

Bregman, S. (2024, July 23). Paris 2024 Olympics: Simone Biles looks sharp and relaxed in practice. Olympics. https://www.olympics.com/en/news/paris-2024-olympics-simone-biles-looks-sharp-and-relaxed-in-practice

Guo, Y., Yuan, T., Peng, J., Deng, L., & Chen, C. (2024). Impact of sports vision training on visuomotor skills and shooting performance in elite skeet shooters. *Frontiers in Human Neuroscience*, 18, 1476649. https://doi.org/10.3389/fnhum.2024.1476649

Ruth, G. H., & Miller, B. (2024). *Babe Ruth's long-lost manual of physical fitness: Including exercises with a bat*. Hudson Society Press.

Strigaro, G., Ruge, D., Chen, J. C., Marshall, L., Desikan, M., Cantello, R., & Rothwell, J. C. (2015). Interaction between visual and motor cortex: A transcranial magnetic stimulation study. *Journal of Physiology*, 593(10), 2365–2377. https://doi.org/10.1113/JP270135

CHAPTER FIVE

Cai, W., Chen, T., Szegletes, L., Supekar, K., & Menon, V. (2018). Aberrant time-varying cross-network interactions in children with attention-deficit/hyperactivity disorder and the relation to attention deficits. *Biological Psychiatry*: Cognitive Neuroscience and Neuroimaging, 3(3), 263–273. https://doi.org/10.1016/j.bpsc.2017.10.005

Gotlieb, R., Yang, X. F., & Immordino-Yang, M. H. (2022). Default and executive networks' roles in diverse adolescents' emotionally engaged construals of complex social issues. *Social Cognitive and Affective Neuroscience*, 17(4), 421–429. https://doi.org/10.1093/scan/nsab108

Kripa, S., & Kaur, H. (2021). Identifying relations between posture and pain in lower back pain patients: A narrative review. *Bulletin of Faculty of Physical Therapy*, 26, 34. https://doi.org/10.1186/s43161-021-00052-w

Schimmelpfennig, J., Topczewski, J., Zajkowski, W., & Jankowiak-Siuda, K. (2023). The role of the salience network in cognitive and affective deficits. *Frontiers in Human Neuroscience*, 17, 1133367. https://doi.org/10.3389/fnhum.2023.1133367

Seeley, W. W. (2019). The salience network: A neural system for perceiving and responding to homeostatic demands. *Journal of Neuroscience*, 39(50), 9878–9882. https://doi.org/10.1523/JNEUROSCI.1138-17.2019

Todd, M. E. (2017). *The thinking body: A study of the balancing forces of dynamic man*. Martino Fine Books. (Original work published 1937)

Xu, J., Van Dam, N. T., Feng, C., Luo, Y., Ai, H., Gu, R., & Xu, P. (2019). Anxious brain networks: A coordinate-based activation likelihood estimation meta-analysis of resting-state functional connectivity studies in anxiety. *Neuroscience & Biobehavioral Reviews*, 96, 21–30. https://doi.org/10.1016/j.neubiorev.2018.11.005

CHAPTER SIX

Bureau of Labor Statistics, U.S. Department of Labor. (2018). Back injuries prominent in work-related musculoskeletal disorder cases in 2016. *The Economics Daily*. Retrieved February 19, 2026, from https://www.bls.gov/opub/ted/2018/back-injuries-prominent-in-work-related-musculoskeletal-disorder-cases-in-2016.htm

Bayram, F., Karatekin, B. D., Erhan, B., Pasin, O., & Yumusakhuylu, Y. (2024). Conservative treatment in adult degenerative scoliosis: A prospective cohort study. *Maedica*, 19(1), 23–29. https://doi.org/10.26574/maedica.2024.19.1.23

Dimitrijević, V., Šćepanović, T., Jevtić, N., Rašković, B., Milankov, V., Milosević, Z., Ninković, S. S., Chockalingam, N., Obradović, B., & Drid, P. (2022). Application of the Schroth method in the treatment of idiopathic scoliosis: A systematic review and meta-analysis. *International Journal of Environmental Research and Public Health*, 19(24), 16730. https://doi.org/10.3390/ijerph192416730

Di Nicola V. (2020). Degenerative osteoarthritis a reversible chronic disease. *Regenerative Therapy*, 15, 149–160. https://doi.org/10.1016/j.reth.2020.07.007

Free Movement Pilates. (n.d.). *About Joseph Pilates*. https://freemovement-pilates.com/about-joseph-pilates

Grubb, J. (2024, November 12). A Pilates history lesson: Joseph Pilates' internment years. *Pilates Intel*. https://www.pilatesintel.com/2024/11/a-pilates-history-lesson-joseph-pilates-internment-years-by-jonathan-grubb/

Heckert, S. L., Maassen, J. M., Nevins, I., Baudoin, P., Steup-Beekman, G. M., Huizinga, T. W. J., Bergstra, S. A., & Allaart, C. F. (2025). Long-term clinical outcomes in early rheumatoid arthritis that was treated-to-target in the BeSt and IMPROVED studies. *Rheumatology*, 64(3), 1052–1059. https://doi.org/10.1093/rheumatology/keae212

Hodges, P. W., Butler, J. E., McKenzie, D. K., & Gandevia, S. C. (1997). Contraction of the human diaphragm during rapid postural adjustments. *The Journal of Physiology*, 505(Pt 2), 539–548. https://doi.org/10.1111/j.1469-7793.1997.539bb.x

Hodges, P., Kaigle Holm, A., Holm, S., Ekström, L., Cresswell, A., Hansson, T., & Thorstensson, A. (2003). Intervertebral stiffness of the spine is increased by evoked contraction of transversus abdominis and the diaphragm: In vivo porcine studies. *Spine*, 28(23), 2594–2601. https://doi.org/10.1097/01.BRS.0000096676.14323.25

Hodges, P. W., & Richardson, C. A. (1996). Inefficient muscular stabilization of the lumbar spine associated with low back pain: A motor control evaluation of transversus abdominis. *Spine*, 21(22), 2640–2650. https://doi.org/10.1097/00007632-199611150-00014

Hodges, P., Richardson, C., & Jull, G. (1996). Evaluation of the relationship between laboratory and clinical tests of transversus abdominis function. *Physiotherapy Research International*, 1(1), 30–40. https://doi.org/10.1002/pri.45

Hodges, P. W., & Richardson, C. A. (1998). Delayed postural contraction of transversus abdominis in low back pain associated with movement of the lower limb. *Journal of Spinal Disorders*, 11(1), 46–56.

Jensen, R. K., Jensen, T. S., Koes, B., & Hartvigsen, J. (2020). Prevalence of lumbar spinal stenosis in general and clinical populations: A systematic review and meta-analysis. *European Spine Journal*, 29(9), 2143–2163. https://doi.org/10.1007/s00586-020-06339-1

Konieczny, M. R., Senyurt, H., & Krauspe, R. (2013). Epidemiology of adolescent idiopathic scoliosis. *Journal of Children's Orthopaedics*, 7(1), 3–9. https://doi.org/10.1007/s11832-012-0457-4

Lindstrom, S. (2026, January 5). Usain Bolt. *Encyclopedia Britannica*. https://www.britannica.com/biography/Usain-Bolt

Longman, J. (2017, July 20). Something strange in Usain Bolt's stride. *The New York Times*. https://www.nytimes.com/2017/07/20/sports/olympics/usain-bolt-stride-speed.html

Martin, B. I., Tosteson, A. N. A., Lurie, J. D., et al. (2014). Back pain in the United States. In *Variation in the care of surgical conditions: Spinal stenosis (A Dartmouth Atlas of Health Care series)*. The Dartmouth Institute for Health Policy and Clinical Practice. https://www.ncbi.nlm.nih.gov/books/NBK586768/

McAviney, J., Roberts, C., Sullivan, B., Alevras, A. J., Graham, P. L., & Brown, B. T. (2020). The prevalence of adult de novo scoliosis: A systematic review and meta-analysis. *European Spine Journal*, 29(12), 2960–2969. https://doi.org/10.1007/s00586-020-06453-0

Nicol, V., Verdaguer, C., Daste, C., Bisseriex, H., Lapeyre, É., Lefèvre-Colau, M.-M., Rannou, F., Rören, A., Facione, J., & Nguyen, C. (2023). Chronic low back pain: A narrative review of recent international guidelines for diagnosis and conservative treatment. *Journal of Clinical Medicine*, 12(4), 1685. https://doi.org/10.3390/jcm12041685

Oliveira, I., Garrido, M. V., & Bernardes, S. F. (2022). On the body-mind nexus in chronic musculoskeletal pain: A scoping review. *European Journal of Pain*, 26(6), 1186–1202. https://doi.org/10.1002/ejp.1944

Sattin, D., Parma, C., Lunetta, C., Zulueta, A., Lanzone, J., Giani, L., Vassallo, M., Picozzi, M., & Parati, E. A. (2023). An overview of the body schema and body image: Theoretical models, methodological settings and pitfalls for rehabilitation of persons with neurological disorders. *Brain Sciences*, 13(10), 1410. https://doi.org/10.3390/brainsci13101410

Wing, C., & Bishop, C. (2020). Hamstring strain injuries: Incidence, mechanisms, risk factors, and training recommendations. *Strength and Conditioning Journal*, 42(3), 40–57. https://doi.org/10.1519/SSC.0000000000000538

CHAPTER SEVEN

Chirico, A., Cipresso, P., Yaden, D. B., et al. (2017). Effectiveness of immersive videos in inducing awe: An experimental study. *Scientific Reports*, 7, 1218. https://doi.org/10.1038/s41598-017-01242-0

Goral, O., Wald, I. Y., Maimon, A., Snir, A., Golland, Y., Goral, A., & Amedi, A. (2024). Enhancing interoceptive sensibility through exteroceptive-interoceptive sensory substitution. *Scientific Reports*, 14(1), 14855. https://doi.org/10.1038/s41598-024-63231-4

Mazziotta, J. (2024, August 2). Simone Biles shares photo of meditative moment before 2024 Olympics all-around win. *People*. https://people.com/simone-biles-shares-photo-meditative-moment-before-2024-olympics-all-around-win-8689633

Puglise, N. (2016, August 8). What is Michael Phelps listening to on his trademark Olympics headphones? *The Guardian*. https://www.theguardian.com/sport/2016/aug/08/michael-phelps-headphones-music-swimming-olympics-rio

Lobenstine, D. M. (2017, October 3). When the massage client is the host: Parasitic tension on the table. *MASSAGE Magazine*. https://www.massage-mag.com/massage-client-host-parasitic-tension-86668/

Siegel, D. J. (2018). Aware: The science and practice of presence. TarcherPerigee.

ABOUT THE AUTHOR

Jenn Pilotti, M.S., has spent more than two decades helping people feel more at home in their bodies. What began as a young trainer's curiosity about why people move the way they do evolved into a career built on a simple conviction: that movement, approached with awareness and honesty, changes everything.

Jenn draws from neuroscience, biomechanics, somatics, motor learning, and over twenty years of working with private clients to create an approach that is as grounded in research as it is in real human experience. She teaches workshops internationally, leads corporate wellness programs, and teaches mindfulness for the U.S. Navy Leadership Seminar. *Spinal Intelligence* is her fourth book.

She lives and moves in Portland, Oregon. You can find her at https://www.jennpilotti.com

www.ingramcontent.com/pod-product-compliance
Lightning Source LLC
Chambersburg PA
CBHW031021160726

47991CB00005B/1819